The Urban School System of the Future

Applying the Principles and Lessons of Chartering

Andy Smarick

ROWMAN & LITTLEFIELD EDUCATION
A division of
ROWMAN & LITTLEFIELD PUBLISHERS, INC.
Lanham • New York • Toronto • Plymouth, UK

Published by Rowman & Littlefield Education
A division of Rowman & Littlefield Publishers, Inc.
A wholly owned subsidary of The Rowman & Littlefield Publishing Group, Inc.
4501 Forbes Boulevard, Suite 200, Lanham, Maryland 20706
www.rowman.com

10 Thornbury Road, Plymouth PL6 7PP, United Kingdom

British Library Cataloguing in Publication Information Available

Library of Congress Cataloging-in-Publication Data

Smarick, Andy.
The urban school system of the future : applying the principles and lessons of chartering / Andy
Smarick.
p. cm.
Includes bibliographical references.
ISBN 978-1-60709-476-0 (hardback) -- ISBN 978-1-60709-477-7 (paper) -- ISBN 978-1-60709-478-
4 (electronic)
1. Education, Urban--United States. 2. Urban schools--United States. 3. Charter schools--United
States. 4. School management and organization--United States. 5. Educational change--United States.
I. Title.
LC5131.S59 2012
370.9173'2--dc23
2012022156

The paper used in this publication meets the minimum requirements of American National
Standard for Information Sciences Permanence of Paper for Printed Library Materials,
ANSI/NISO Z39.48-1992.

Printed in the United States of America

Contents

List of Figures

Introduction

Chapter 3

Chapter 6

Chapter 7

Chapter 9

Chapter 10

Acknowledgments

I am indebted to a number of individuals and organizations for their generous support. Scott Hamilton, Bruno Manno, Marc Porter Magee, Tom Vander Ark, and Todd Ziebarth read and offered helpful comments on the manuscript. Chester Finn and Mike Petrilli of the Thomas B. Fordham Institute and Rick Hess of the American Enterprise Institute were excellent colleagues and provided moral support, rewarding side projects, and a gratifying professional home during my blissful government-service interregnum.

The Aspen Institute provided an idyllic place to write and, through its NewSchools fellowship program, invaluable professional development and lifelong friends and colleagues in the Agitators. The willingness of the editors of *EducationNext* to publish the contrarian articles "Wave of the Future" and "The Turnaround Fallacy," which serve as this book's foundation, encouraged my thinking about systemic reform when other subjects were the vogue.

Two anonymous Catholic dioceses provided otherwise impossible-to-obtain data on their schools' test scores and poverty levels, which significantly benefited this book's third section. The Walton Family Foundation's support for and Roman & Littlefield's partnership in this project are both greatly appreciated. Though I'm certain all of the above wouldn't want to be associated with everything in the pages that follow, whatever value this book has is attributable to their collective smarts and support.

Finally, and most importantly, I am eternally grateful to my wife Kathie, without whom this book would not be. She remained enormously, even inexplicably, encouraging, from my hesitant proposal of a book-writing sabbatical through three years of writing and the birth of three children. A writer, husband, and father couldn't be more fortunate.

Introduction

The traditional urban public school system is broken, and it cannot be fixed. It must be replaced. In the pages to come I offer an explanation for the seemingly unshakeable struggles of our inner-city public schools and a road map for meaningful, lasting improvement.

Anyone setting about to improve urban education obviously faces a colossal task, but today's education writer bears a particular burden. He must explain what in the world another book will accomplish. Over the last several decades, barrels of ink have been spilled on the subject. This is well-traveled territory by now so new trails—a book's reason for being—are tough to blaze.

Moreover, the growing conventional wisdom holds that new ideas are more of a distraction than a contribution; solving our problems, it's now widely believed, simply requires political courage and faithful implementation of a set of consensus reforms. On both scores my take is entirely different. First, today's most popular reform strategies, like improved data use and human capital initiatives, will never result in the improvements we so desperately need. They are certainly necessary, but they are miles from sufficient.

Second, I am convinced that the *only* path to success is through a wholly new understanding of the problem and a significantly different approach to reform.

Just about everyone working in the realm of urban education, from teachers and researchers to foundation leaders and nonprofit-based reformers, assumes that the traditional school district is essential and immortal—that because of its age and standing, it must be the driver of and/or the focus of reform.

My argument is that the district is not part of the solution; it is the problem. Persistent low performance is the natural consequence of this institution that our predecessors placed at the heart of urban public schooling. No city will ever realize a renaissance in K–12 education so long as the district continues as the dominant, default delivery system for public education. The replacement must be a new "system of schools," governed by the revolutionary practices of chartering. By using four innovations introduced into public education by chartering, we can create dynamic, responsive, high-performing, self-improving urban school systems.

Though this new system will require the demotion of the district and the development of a new citywide education authority, neither shift will be as dramatic or disruptive as it may first appear. The district will merely become one of a range of co-equal providers. It will still be able to operate schools, but it won't hold a privileged place in the landscape. The new system's guiding principles will apply to the district's schools in the same way as other providers' schools.

The new authority, the Office of the Chancellor of City Schools, will be a relatively small entity. It will neither operate nor authorize schools. It will execute the system's four principles—diversity of options, new starts, replications/expansions, and closures—acting as the citywide "portfolio manager" of schools.

In many ways, the new system will look and behave like the healthy industries so common in the private sector. Quality, consumer choice, a wide array of alternatives, and innovation will play much larger roles than in today's district-dominated arrangement. However, the system will not be a freewheeling marketplace. There will be public management and public oversight, and it will carefully preserve the key elements of public education, such as universal access, open enrollment, and non-discrimination.

Once operational, this new system of schools will not only deliver improved results, it will also feel extraordinarily familiar: For years, other critically important government functions have been carried out in the manner recommended here. Through these changes we'll soon come to realize just how anomalous and deeply flawed our previous urban public school system actually was.

THE DISTRICT AS THE SYSTEM

The term "urban school system" is terribly misleading, and this is far more than semantics. In fact, it neatly captures the problem at the center of U.S. urban public education. "System" normally refers to numerous moving parts working together to form an integrated whole. The traditional urban school "system" is no such thing. Instead, the district is a monolith. For decades and decades in all of our major cities, the district was the sole owner and operator of all public schools. Every public school in the city belonged to it, and it controlled every aspect of those schools. The district, this lone, hulking organization, became synonymous with public education.

This last point proved to be especially problematic because it served to obscure a crucial set of facts. It's simply not the case that a single delivery system had to define public schooling; the principles of public education could be carried out in any number of ways. Furthermore, there's nothing to say that the district had to be one of these ways. In fact, the district was born of the particular events, beliefs, and politics of a specific historical period.

The decades around the turn of the twentieth century were marked by industrialization and mass immigration. America's cities grew crowded, and poverty and other problems mounted. The existing public schools were too few to match the burgeoning demand, and they were ill-equipped to deal with the growing challenges of the time. Across the nation, ascendant progressives sought to replace the messy machine politics of the day with cleaner, more professional good government. Their strategies were informed by a fondness for a relatively new player on the economic stage, the large corporation.

Though their shortcomings would become apparent in the decades to come, corporations had great appeal at the time, especially among those seeking to improve urban education. They not only earned impressive profits, created jobs, and accomplished difficult tasks, they were also rationally organized and—especially as they became vertically integrated—extremely efficient. The progressives also believed in elevating the city's "best men," leading figures in academia and industry, to positions of political power. These pillars of the community would rise above petty politics and ably advance the public good.

The combination of these principles led to the creation of the district, which, in city after city, came to dominate public education. A school board, like a corporate board of directors, would be populated by respected city leaders and provide governance. The superintendency would be filled by a trusted executive who would lead operations like a CEO. The large, centralized bureaucracy would fully control the city's public schools, providing continuity and stability, achieving economies of scale, rooting out nepotism, and delivering consistent offerings and results.

For a number of reasons, this little-known history must become part of today's discussions. First, the district's creation was anything but inevitable. Had immigration's peak not coincided with the progressives' rise, had machine politics not temporarily given neighborhood control of schools a bad name, or had the public realized sooner the dangers of large, vertically aligned monopolies, the district may have never come into being.

Moreover, while the rest of the world has evolved in staggering ways over the last hundred years, the urban district, amazingly, has gone virtually unchanged. It has aged and ossified. Education historians Diane Ravitch and Joseph Viteritti aptly described it as the "decrepit factory."[1] But most importantly, the district has generated heartbreakingly poor results for generations.

Put together, these points compel us to question the district's long-protected status and wonder if something else is possible. But the final point is especially pregnant. Perhaps the failings of urban public education and the district structure are knit into a single fabric. For years some reformers, particularly those on the right, have made this case, arguing there is a strong link between urban education's institutional arrangements and its low performance. Because the district is a monopoly, they've argued, it will always inflate costs and produce suboptimal results, even if run by the "best men."

It's tough to disagree with this assessment. The urban school district *was designed* as a monopoly, monopolies have certain undesirable characteristics, and urban districts exhibit those unwanted traits. But this book treats the monopoly answer as incomplete for two reasons. First, when urban districts have had to face competition via private and/or public school choice programs, they haven't drastically improved their performance. In many cases, they seem to have not improved at all.

Second, if our ultimate goal is to build an environment that ensures that all of a city's students have access to great schools, then the "the-monopoly-is-the-problem" argument leaves today's policymaker with entirely too many unanswered questions. It doesn't tell us what the new role of the district will be. It doesn't tell us how to ensure quality across all schools. It doesn't tell us how the supply of schools will be managed. In short, it fails to address the question implied at the beginning of this section: What should be our *system* for schools?

The case made here is that this question can only be answered by understanding how the district's standing as a monolithic, corporation-like organization prevents urban public education from possessing the characteristics of a healthy industry. Even a cursory appreciation of how successful fields and industries function reveals some of the district's shortcomings. But the picture becomes crystal clear by applying the lessons of Richard Foster and Sarah Kaplan's landmark 2001 book *Creative Destruction.*[2]

Marshalling decades of data, Foster and Kaplan show that industries always outperform even the very best corporations. The dynamic process of "creative destruction," where new firms emerge, existing ones compete, failing ones disappear, and successful ones grow, guarantees system-wide success and improvement over time. A single corporation might succeed for a period, but the healthy churn surrounding it will always generate better results. Ultimately, even a once-dominant firm will falter, become obsolete, get lapped by the field, and close or get taken over. Said simply, *an entity can't compete with a strong system.*

For urban education, the implications are tremendous. Basing the delivery mechanism of urban public schooling on a corporation was precisely wrong. The district's ubiquity, continuity, stability, and uniformity may have seemed sensible in 1900. But these characteristics are lethal if high performance and continuous improvement are the goal. The district's replacement must be a system that generates the dynamism of a thriving industry.

This means we must develop an entirely new approach to managing a city's collection of schools. The approach must include strategies for addressing new schools, great schools, and failing schools. Even more importantly, it means challenging a core feature of the district mentality, a conviction held dear by many in the education establishment: that a single government entity must own and operate all of a city's schools.

GOVERNMENT SERVICES THROUGH MULTIPLE PROVIDERS

Today, seldom is the district's structure defended on progressive grounds—that its corporate-like, monopolistic form is prudent and orderly. A far more common defense is that, first, for public education to be truly public, all public schools must be owned and operated by the government and, second, it's rational to vest this authority in a single entity.

This line of argument, however, runs counter to both the best thinking on and our daily experience with the delivery of government services. Nearly twenty years ago David Osborne and Ted Gaebler made a groundbreaking argument about how government should do its business in their book *Reinventing Government.*[3] Summarizing the shortcomings of government generally, not just regarding public education, they wrote, "The kind of governments that developed during the industrial era, with their sluggish, centralized bureaucracies, their preoccupation with rules and regulations, and their hierarchical chains of command, no longer work very well."

They offered as an alternative "entrepreneurial government," where the government ensures that important things get accomplished while allowing others to do most of the day-to-day work. In such a system, the government would "steer" the ship, while the "third sector" (primarily nonprofits) would "row." The authors identified another key failing of that previous era's approach to government. "The progressive confidence in 'neutral administrators' and 'professionalism' blinded us to the consequences of taking control out of the hands of families and communities." Government becomes slow, focused on inputs, and indifferent to consumer needs.

A better system, they argued, would allow trusted, established community organizations to deliver services and would empower families to select among providers. This decentralization of power would enable service deliverers to focus on mission and outcomes and turn citizens into customers able to exercise choice.

In recent years, a number of scholars and practitioners have built on the themes in *Reinventing Government*, most prominently former Indianapolis mayor Stephen Goldsmith. In *The Power of Social Innovation*, Goldsmith, with co-authors Gigi Georges and Tim Glynn Burke, argue that government too often convinces itself that it knows best how to deliver services.[4] Then through politics and regulation, it insulates itself from competition. The result is low performance and a jealously guarded status quo.

Their prescription is similar to Osborne and Gaebler's: The government should see that public value is produced primarily by building systems that ensure that work is accomplished and outcomes are high-quality. It should remove itself, however, from the business of controlling the means of producing public value and accomplishing results. Instead, an array of civic entrepreneurs should offer a range of options to consumers.

Similarly, in *Unlocking the Power of Networks*, Goldsmith with Donald F. Kettl discuss the new "networked government" that has evolved from the reconsideration of how government goes about its work.[5] Today, "Government social service programs ripple out through a huge collection of non-profit community-based organizations." The list of activities once owned by the government but now taken on by other providers includes public works, urban development, public housing, mental health, welfare, crime prevention, libraries, fire protection, and more.

A large part of the draw of these new arrangements, according to Goldsmith and Kettl, is that networked government decentralizes authority and enables evolution; the system adapts to new conditions and responds with improvements in quality.

So how should we connect these many threads in a way that leads to better schools for disadvantaged kids in urban America? Namely, how do we transition from a monolith to a system? How do we shift the government's role in education from rowing to primarily steering? How do we empower the expansive and diverse "third sector" to deliver this essential public service? How do we put power back in the hands of families and communities? How do we ensure that the new system smartly addresses new schools, failing schools, and exceptional schools, bringing about the continuous improvement and healthy churn of dynamic industries?

CHARTERING AS THE SYSTEM

The answer to all of these questions—and the blueprint for the urban school system of the future—can be found in charter schooling. The systemic innovation of chartering has already shown that the government need not be the exclusive operator of all public schools. A wide array of organizations can deliver a public education, creating a public schools marketplace.

Chartering has also already demonstrated that there can be variety and churn within public education: Diverse new schools can be continually created, failing schools can be closed, and great schools can be replicated and expanded. What remains to be seen is whether these revolutionary characteristics can form the core of a comprehensive and coherent new public education system. This book argues it can and explains how.

The key is moving the government away from rowing and toward steering. At a high level, this means—in language echoing Osborne, Gaebler, and Goldsmith—that government sees to it that public value is produced by creating a system that allows others to produce it. More specifically, this means shifting urban governments primarily into the business of managing portfolios of schools operated by others. But in order to realize the full benefits of this new type of system, we need a drastic change in perspective, an intellectual leap that few, even among the most daring reformers, have been willing to take.

To the extent that the public education establishment has accepted chartering, it is an enervated interpretation of chartering. The mechanism is seen as a way to create a handful of autonomous public schools. If it is credited with having created a new sector within public education, that sector is certainly thought to be on the periphery, an auxiliary. If chartering is recognized as having any systemic influence, it is as an R&D arm, a means of developing and testing new ideas that will then be shared with the real system—the district.

Unfortunately, this view has been adopted, at least tacitly, by most of the education reform community. The leading human-capital nonprofits focus their energies on districts. Leading foundations' major initiatives do likewise. This is not to say that chartering is ignored, only that it is treated as subsidiary. The leap essential to the fundamental improvement of urban public education has two components.

First, we must see chartering not as a sector and not even as *a* system but as *the* system for urban education's future. The systemic practices it has introduced into public education must be the playbook for how urban school portfolios are managed. Second, we must accept that the full flourishing of this new system requires the permanent demotion and the potential cessation of the district.

When put so bluntly, these two intertwined ideas might seem extreme. But in fact they are the logical extension of the best thinking about structural reform and the most exciting developments in urban education over the last two decades. In other words, while this book's recommendations certainly push the envelope, they have a twenty-year pedigree in thought and action.

Ted Kolderie was one of the originators of the charter schooling concept and in the years since has done as much as anyone to change the debate about the delivery of public education. His apt description of school districts as "exclusive territorial franchises" was among the first and most influential criticisms of the progressives' central education legacy. Kolderie's subsequent arguments in favor of an "open sector" of public schools presaged numerous policies and practices that led to the creation of new schools, the replication of successful models, and the diversification of public school offerings.[6]

Equally important has been Paul Hill of the University of Washington. His early advocacy for contracting was a frontal assault on the district's primary role as an operator of schools. In recent years, Hill and his colleagues at the Center on Reinventing Public Education have been among the strongest backers of some districts' move from education provider to portfolio manager.[7]

These ideas have made their way into practice in important ways. The most obvious is charter schooling itself. No longer can districts claim to have a proprietary right to public education. Now, in most cities, a diverse assortment of nonprofits operate public schools. Moreover, chartering has shown that the key practices advocated for here can work in public education. A diversity of new schools can be started from scratch. Low-performing schools can be closed. Great schools can be replicated.

Importantly, these ideas have spread beyond the charter sector. A few forward-thinking district leaders have embraced new starts, closures, and replications. To varying extents, these strategies have been put to work in Baltimore, Chicago, Detroit, and more. As noteworthy, a growing number of district leaders have begun talking about "a system of schools" instead of a "school system." And in the cases of New York City and New Orleans— thanks to the extraordinary leadership, respectively, of former chancellor Joel Klein and former state superintendent Paul Pastorek—nearly all of the pieces have been put in place.

Despite this progress, most leaders in the establishment and reform community still fail to recognize that chartering represents a systemic solution. When speaking of a "system of schools," their emphasis is on *schools* not *system*. Many believe that the key is empowering of principals; that is, they prioritize the shift from centralized control to site-based management. But this is a small piece of the puzzle. It is possible for a city to have completely independent but dreadfully low-performing schools. School-based autonomy is ultimately meaningless to the system unless there are sensible, consistent consequences for different levels of performance.

Furthermore, many of those who profess to see the value of new starts, closures, and/or replications still fail to appreciate that these strategies must be applied on an ongoing and coordinated basis, not merely as a one-time kick-start. Closing schools isn't just a way to right-size a district that's lost enrollment; it's the way to continuously shed failing programs. A regular new-schools program ensures that a city's portfolio is continually adjusted to match evolving needs. A consistent replication effort guarantees that the best offerings are always grown.

But the most portentous error made by even those sympathetic to this book's main arguments is a continued reliance on the district as the central actor. Those who have written in support of portfolio management invariably assume that the district will become the manager. In the cities where this strategy has taken root, the district is in the lead role.

But the district was created to be a monopoly owner and operator of schools, not an impartial assessor of a landscape of schools run by others. The district's longstanding job has been codified in laws, regulations, and other policies. As importantly, the district has developed innumerable beliefs and practices to support this line of work. We can't expect a century-old organization to completely change its fundamental nature. No one would try to turn General Electric into General Mills.

Moreover, the urban district is quite simply a failed organization. It has done an astonishingly poor job at its primary task, running schools. Why in the world would we think an organization that's extraordinarily bad at its job would be great at another? The work of revitalizing urban education is far too important to give the district the central role.

The answer is to create from scratch a new entity that will manage a city's schools portfolio. In recognition of the district's current role as the primary operator of schools, it would be allowed to continue doing so for the time being. But its future would not be guaranteed; instead, it would be a function of the district's performance. In other words, the district's fate would be in its own hands. If it can run high-performing schools, it will live on; it may even enlarge its market share. But if its schools continue to fail, they will be closed, and the district will ultimately work itself out of business if others do a better job.

MANAGING THE PORTFOLIO OF SCHOOLS

The arguments outlined above and the arrangement of this book flow from a few straightforward principles. The first is that our overarching goal ought to be constantly growing the number of city kids who attend high-performing schools. Implicit in this statement is what might be called "sector agnosticism," complete ambivalence about who runs a great school and with which sector it is associated. This approach eschews the central battle of urban education politics, where decision-makers align themselves with traditional public schools, charter public schools, or private schools and then war with those from the other camps.

I have equal affection for great traditional public schools, great charter public schools, and great private schools. I am equally opposed to the low-performers from each sector. Basing a reform strategy on this tack, I strongly believe, is the right philosophical approach. But it also reflects what the data tell us. Each of the first three sections of this book is dedicated to one of the three sectors. In addition to providing important historical context, each section has performance results from each group of schools. In city after city, we see that each sector has a widely distributed bell curve of quality. And those curves look startlingly similar.

Regardless of what urban area you are in, there are some high-performing charters, district schools, and private schools. And there are middling performers and low performers from each as well. The graphic representation (Figure 0.1) of this phenomenon won't surprise anyone who has taken an introductory statistics course. But it will, I hope, reorient the debate; it shows the senselessness of our sector-focused approach. We shouldn't fight over which curve is slightly farther to the right, meaning which curve has a slightly higher mean performance level, because the mean is meaningless. It masks the enormous variation under the curve.

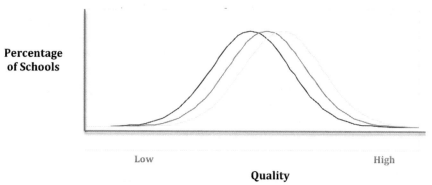

Figure 0.1

Instead, we should have strategies for schools on the right side of the distribution, on the left side, and in the middle. This is the conceptual foundation for portfolio management and the principles of chartering.

I show, however, that the central argument of this book is supported by more than theory. In the places where these strategies are being faithfully implemented, most notably in New Orleans and New York City, the results are powerfully positive. Not only is the system envisioned here possible, it's producing the gains in student learning that we all desire.

The first section focuses on the traditional urban school district. Chapter 1 shows that this system has failed, for generations, to prepare students in America's cities for success. Chapter 2 details the massive efforts to improve the district system, which have combined to generate amazingly little.

Chapter 3 introduces the quality distribution concept and argues for a new way of approaching reform. The final chapter of the first section argues that our primary strategy for addressing the quality distribution challenge, efforts to turn around persistently underperforming schools, has been, and will continue to be, an utter failure.

The second section begins with an historical look at chartering and an introduction to the ideas at the heart of this book. Chapter 6 mirrors chapter 3 but applies the analysis to the charter sector and then shows what can be accomplished through faithful implementation of portfolio management. Chapter 7, the book's core, explains the four innovations of chartering and details how they can inform portfolio management and lead to the development of the urban school system of the future.

Private schooling is the subject of the third section. Chapter 8 describes private education's evolving relationship with the public system and begins the argument that portfolio management ought to be applied to all three sectors. Chapter 9 shows that the private schools sector has a quality distribution similar to traditional public schools and charter schools.

The final section describes the urban school system of the future. Chapter 10 details the steps necessary for building this new system and how policies and practices can be changed to drive continuous improvement. Chapter 11 concludes the book by arguing that the new system is within close reach but still must be pursued with great care and persistence.

NOTES

1. Diane Ravitch and Joseph P. Viteritti, "Introduction," in *New Schools for a New Century: The Redesign of Urban Education*, eds. Diane Ravitch and Joseph P. Viteritti (New Haven, CT: Yale University Press, 1999).

2. Richard Foster and Sarah Kaplan, *Creative Destruction: Why Companies That Are Built to Last Underperform the Market—And How to Successfully Transform Them* (New York: Broadway Business, 2004).

3. David Osborne and Ted Gaebler, *Reinventing Government: How the Entrepreneurial Spirit is Transforming the Public Sector* (New York: Plume, 1993).

4. Stephen Goldsmith, with Gigi Georges and Tim Glynn Burke, *The Power of Social Innovation: How Civic Entrepreneurs Ignite Community Networks for Good* (San Francisco: Jossey-Bass, 2010).

5. Stephen Goldsmith and Donald F. Kettl, *Unlocking the Power of Networks: Keys to High-Performance Government* (Washington, DC: Brookings Institution Press, 2009).

6. Ted Kolderie, *Creating the Capacity for Change: How and Why Governors and Legislatures Are Opening a New-Schools Sector in Public Education.* (Bethesda, MD: Education Week Press, 2004).

7. See Paul Hill and James W. Guthrie, *Reinventing Public Education: How Contracting Can Transform America's Schools* (Chicago: University of Chicago Press, 1997); Paul Hill, Christine Campbell, and James Harvey, *It Takes a City: Getting Serious About Urban School Reform* (Washington, DC: Brookings Institution Press, 2000); and Paul Hill, et al., *Portfolio School Districts for Big Cities*, Interim Report (Bothell: Center for Reinventing Public Education, University of Washington, October 2009).

Part I

The Traditional Urban School District

Chapter 1

The Failure of the Urban District

THE ROLE OF PUBLIC EDUCATION IN AMERICA'S CITIES

Our country's public schools exist to provide a high-quality education to all students, regardless of their wealth, race, or mailing address. Though public education is now a given in the world's developed nations, this idea of free, accessible, high-performing K–12 schools has a particularly American flair. It speaks to our sense of justice, opportunity, and equality—that all boys and girls are equally filled with promise and that their prospects for health and happiness should be boundless.

It is in this context that we must consider our system of urban public education. In order for disadvantaged kids growing up in these communities to reach early adulthood fully prepared to excel in college and career, their schools must be academically rigorous, stable, safe, and more. Admittedly, these are titanic demands. Their students often enter school academically underprepared; neighborhood conditions frequently inhibit their progress; and too often the policies and politics surrounding their work are inhospitable to academic success.

Yet the enormity of this challenge neither lessens schools' charge nor excuses their inability to live up to it. While cataloguing the difficulties these schools face might alleviate the consternation of the adults running them, doing so doesn't improve the life chances of their students. Kids don't become better readers when others lament the chips stacked against them. They don't learn algebra when fingers are pointed at their parents. With this in mind, we can ask the question squarely: Though much is asked of them, are our urban districts providing a high-quality education to their students? By any measure, the answer is an unqualified no.

CONTEMPORARY RESULTS

The National Assessment of Educational Progress (NAEP), known widely as the "Nation's Report Card," has provided national- and state-level test scores for years. But more recently, NAEP began sampling a number of urban districts to determine how the academic results of their students compared to other students around the country. The findings are alarming.

As of 2007, only 20 percent of New York City's eighth graders could read proficiently. In Houston, Chicago, Los Angeles, and Atlanta the scores were even lower. In Cleveland, the lowest performing of the cities sampled, only one in ten eighth graders read at the proficient level. In math, the results were similarly shocking. In Washington, D.C., only 8 percent of eighth graders reached proficiency.

The results of state-level exams confirm the crisis. In 2000, California released its first ranking of public schools based on the state's "Academic Performance Index." The lowest performing 20 percent of the state's schools were concentrated in its big urban school districts. About 40 percent of the state's worst schools were in ten districts that comprised only 19 percent of the state's schools. More than half of Los Angeles' schools fell in the bottom quintile of state performance.[1]

In the 2007–8 school year, more than half of the schools in Chicago, Detroit, Los Angeles, and Philadelphia failed to make "adequate yearly progress" (AYP), the floor for acceptable school improvement. In the nation's capital, less than 25 percent of schools made AYP. A study by the U.S. Department of Education found that in 2005–6, urban schools were more than twice as likely as suburban schools and three times as likely as rural schools to be identified for improvement under state accountability systems.[2]

Moreover, many of these schools fail to reach their academic targets year after year. As of 2009, more than a third of the schools in Detroit were in "improvement status," having missed AYP for two years in a row or more. In Los Angeles alone, nearly four-hundred thousand students attended schools that were in No Child Left Behind (NCLB) improvement status.

In most cases, these schools are poorly serving the vast majority of their students. In 2006–7, 85 percent of Baltimore schools that missed AYP did so because of the "all students" category. By comparison, nationwide, only 43 percent of schools missing AYP missed because of the "all students" category. Most disturbing are the schools that are in a persistent state of failure. In 2009, one out of five schools in Baltimore and Philadelphia were in "restructuring implementation," the most serious level of intervention under NCLB, indicating at least six years of underperformance.

In New York City, 191 schools were either planning or implementing a federally required restructuring intervention; in Chicago, 235 schools had such plans. The human toll is staggering: in the nation's three largest school districts, New York City, Los Angeles, and Chicago, nearly six-hundred thousand students attended schools in restructuring status.[3]

While there are struggling schools everywhere, our urban schools are particularly troubled. Poor urban schools are much likelier than poor rural schools and poor suburban schools to be required by federal law to provide additional educational options to their students.[4]

City schools are also significantly overrepresented among the universe of schools facing the most severe federal interventions. One study found that 60 percent of the schools in California facing restructuring were located in urban areas. In Michigan, it was 84 percent; in Maryland, 85 percent; in Ohio, 92 percent.[5] A heartbreaking consequence is the soaring dropout rate in our cities. In the school systems encompassing the nation's fifty largest cities, only 52 percent of students graduate high school with a diploma. In Indianapolis, it was 31 percent; in Detroit, the city with the lowest rate, only 25 percent of students graduated.[6]

Not only do our urban schools drastically underperform other American schools, they also underperform schools across the globe. The average U.S. student in a large central city performed statistically below the average of twelve industrialized nations. Eighth graders in Cleveland and Washington, D.C., performed at the same level as students in Macedonia and the Philippines and were outperformed by students in Bulgaria, Armenia, and Serbia.[7]

Interestingly, a survey found that these problems shouldn't be blamed solely on disengaged families. Parents of disadvantaged American students are well aware of the world's changing economic landscape. Two-thirds of low-income parents—a higher rate than among moderate- and high-income parents—said that the things students need to learn today are very different compared to twenty years ago. And Hispanic and African-American parents were more likely to agree with that statement than their white counterparts.[8]

Fully 92 percent of African-American parents and 90 percent of Hispanic parents believe that a K–12 education that prepares their children for college was very important. These rates are higher than for white parents. In most cases, their high expectations are matched by their high awareness of the shortcomings of their schools. While three-quarters of parents with children in low-performing schools believe that preparation for college is very important, only 18 percent of those parents believe their schools are doing the job adequately.

Possibly the most disquieting aspect of this crisis is that there aren't examples of major city districts consistently educating most of their students well. The Broad Prize for Urban Education illustrates this point. Established by the Broad Foundation in 2002 to draw attention to the best in urban education, the prize is awarded annually to the city district demonstrating the greatest student performance, improvement in achievement, and progress toward reducing the achievement gap.

In Houston, Boston, and New York City, the winners in 2002, 2006, and 2007 respectively, less than one-quarter of eighth graders reach proficiency on the NAEP reading exam. Each has a reading proficiency rate that is statistically the same as the average U.S. large central city and each falls well below the nationwide average. Each drastically underperforms its statewide average; in Boston, an eighth grader is about half as likely to be a proficient reader as a peer elsewhere in Massachusetts. These are the best urban districts the nation has to offer.

LONGSTANDING UNDERPERFORMANCE

We can't forget that this crisis has gone on for decades. A series of interrelated demographic shifts throughout the first half of the twentieth century increased poverty rates and the concentration of minority populations in urban areas. In a 1964 college commencement address outlining his agenda, President Johnson explained that two of the three areas of focus for the "Great Society" would be the nation's cities and its classrooms.

Lamenting the "catalogue of ills" facing America's cities, Johnson argued for the need to "rebuild the entire urban United States" and improve schooling with the conviction that "poverty must not be a bar to learning, and learning must offer an escape from poverty." Though the 1965 Elementary and Secondary Education Act (ESEA) directed the federal government's resources toward struggling schools, an inconspicuous directive in the 1964 Civil Rights Act ultimately provided the intellectual underpinnings for the next half century's work on low-income schools.

The law required a study on the educational opportunities available to children of different backgrounds, leading, two years later, to the publication of the "Equality of Education Opportunity Study." Known widely as the Coleman Report, named after lead researcher James Coleman, the study found that the things schools can't control (e.g., race and income) have more influence on student performance, and school inputs (e.g., class size and funding) have less influence, than previously thought.

If our premise is that public schooling's purpose is to provide an excellent education to students regardless of their backgrounds, then the report told us not that schools don't matter but that most urban schools were not mattering enough. A number of variables were depressing the achievement of some students, those variables were prevalent in urban areas, and the public schools serving those students weren't compensating.

The Coleman Report didn't require the reader to believe that urban school districts were malicious, just that most of their schools were not up to the tough task to which they were assigned. In the years that followed, the story remained the same. In a special education message to Congress in 1970, President Nixon wrote, "The outcome of schooling—what children learn—is profoundly different for different groups of children and different parts of the country...We do not have equal educational opportunity in America."

Later that decade, just as state-level "minimum competency testing" was gaining traction, SAT scores began showing the yawning achievement gap between students of different races and economic backgrounds. During the same period, urban teachers were unionizing and striking, middle class families were fleeing to the suburbs, and courts were requiring forced busing, all testifying to the deteriorating condition of urban education.

At the same time, proposals for vouchers and charter schools—educational alternatives for low-income families—were gaining steam. By the early 1990s, Milwaukee had the first publicly funded scholarship program, and charters were already opening in Minneapolis and Los Angeles.

Frustrated that their cities were unable to fix their schools, a number of states orchestrated district takeovers. New Jersey took control of Newark's schools. Pennsylvania and Missouri assumed authority of Philadelphia's and St. Louis's schools. Michigan intervened in the operations and finances of Detroit's schools. In other instances, state legislators, unconvinced that state education departments were any better equipped to fix troubled schools than districts, turned to mayors. In Chicago, New York City, Boston, Baltimore, and Washington, D.C., mayors were given greater authority over schools' daily operations.

EXPLANATION FOR THE CRISIS

This continued failure has engendered a raft of explanations. The most prominent of these relate to the "out-of-school" factors highlighted in the Coleman Report. Lead poisoning and low birth weight, both more prevalent among the low-income, can inhibit cognitive development in children. Poor parents have decreased rates of formal education and read to their children less often than affluent parents, adversely affecting early learning.

Research has found that impoverished environments may stunt the brain development of adolescents and that living in public housing has a negative effect on student learning. The consequences of these obstacles are seen at the earliest stages of schooling. Poor four-year-olds are much less likely than their more affluent peers to have important pre-reading and pre-math skills.

Many argue that this has a spiraling effect: Low-income, mostly minority urban students perform poorly in school and then, unable to thrive financially, raise children in the same achievement-hindering environments. Research by the Brookings Institution on economic mobility found that 54 percent of African-American children born into the bottom economic quintile end up in the same status as adults.[9]

Some academics have offered more incendiary explanations, centered on natural capacity. Nearly a hundred years ago, a college president, arguing against the necessity of a college-preparatory secondary education for "the great army of incapables," pointed to the "dullards" and "subnormal children," "whose mental development heredity decrees a slow pace and early arrest."[10]

Almost a century later, two prominent social scientists, Charles Murray and Richard Herrnstein, published the polarizing *The Bell Curve*, which argued that the differences in native intelligence among different racial groups explain class differences and more.[11] Consequently, some hold low expectations for their students. A number of studies have reported on the paucity of assignments given to, and the low level of the work demanded of, disadvantaged students.[12]

Some observers argue that were urban education better funded, schools could help overcome these forces. Title I of ESEA and large increases in state investments were the result of poor cities' inability to sufficiently support their schools. Others believe the system is the problem, arguing that a city school district has all of the characteristics of a monopoly and suffers the predictable consequences.

For decades, urban school boards had an exclusive right to provide K–12 education. They ran all of the schools, owned all buildings, and employed all staff. Most parents, unable to afford private school tuition or the cost of relocating to a higher-performing district, were left without alternatives. As a result, some claim, city school systems' performance fell while costs increased. Some single out collective bargaining agreements, arguing that the growing unionization and painful strikes of the 1960s and 1970s expanded the influence of teachers' unions, leading to labor contracts that served the interests of employees not students.

John Chubb and Terry Moe, in the seminal 1990 *Politics, Markets, and America's Schools*, pulled together these strands and offered a new explanation: that democratic control of public education inevitably leads to interest groups' power over decision-making. System-wide bureaucratization results, which inhibits the proper functioning of schools. Education scholar Ted Kolderie's 2004 *Creating the Capacity for Change* also blames systemic arrangements, arguing that the diverse educational needs of a community cannot be met by a single provider running a static set of schools.

Those offering similar "the system is the problem" explanations typically offer a similar set of solutions based around greater choice, competition, and flexibility. Nobel prize-winning economist Milton Friedman and Chubb and Moe sought to empower families with vouchers to expand the supply of schools from which families could choose and generate competitive pressure on public schools. Kolderie has argued for an "open sector" in which public entities are able to create new and different types of schools outside of the district structure.

Given the scope and duration of our urban school problems, it's unsurprising that so many explanations have been offered. But this has caused problems, because there is no consensus on the correct course of action, and some of the most strongly advocated reform strategies are mutually exclusive. But if there is a silver lining, it's that the longevity of our urban district problems has provided the opportunity to test the various recommendations as we search for an answer. These numerous and diverse efforts and their consistently disappointing results are at the heart of chapter 2.

NOTES

1. *California's Lowest-Performing Schools: Who They Are, the Challenges They Face, and How They're Improving* (Palo Alto, CA: EdSource, February 2003), 1.
2. U.S. Department of Education, Institute of Education Sciences, *National Assessment of Title I: Final Report, Summary of Key Findings* (Washington, DC: National Center for Educational Evaluation and Regional Assistance, October 2007), 12.
3. Data available in Consolidated State Performance Reports, U.S. Department of Education, http://www2.ed.gov/admins/lead/account/consolidated/index.html.
4. U.S. Department of Education, Office of Planning, Evaluation and Policy Development, Policy and Program Studies Service, *State and Local Implementation of the No Child Left Behind Act, Volume VII—Title I School Choice and Supplemental Educational Services: Final Report* (Jessup, MD: Education Publications Center, U.S. Department of Education, 2009), 10–11.
5. Caitlin Scott, *A Call to Restructure Restructuring: Lessons from the No Child Left Behind Act in Five States* (Washington, DC: Center for Education Policy, 2008).
6. Christopher Swanson, "Cities in Crisis: A Special Analytical Report on High School Graduation" (Bethesda, MD: Editorial Projects in Education, 2008).
7. Gary W. Phillips and John A. Dossey, "Counting on the Future: International Benchmarks in Mathematics for American School Districts" (Washington, DC: American Institutes for Research, 2008).
8. John M. Bridgeland, et al. "One Dream, Two Realities: Perspectives of Parents on America's High Schools" (Washington, DC: Civic Enterprises, 2008), http://www.eric.ed.gov/PDFS/ED503358.pdf.
9. Julia B. Isaacs, "Economic Mobility of Black and White Families," in *Getting Ahead or Losing Ground: Economic Mobility in America,* eds. Julia B. Isaacs, Isabel V. Sawhill, and Ron Haskins (Washington, DC: Brookings Institution and Economic Mobility Project, 2008), 71–80.

10. G. Stanley Hall, *Adolescence: Its Psychology and its Relations to Physiology, Anthropology, Sociology, Sex, Crime, Religion, and Education, v. 2* (New York: Appleton, 1904), 510: quoted in Diane Ravitch, *Left Back: A Century of Failed School Reforms* (New York: Simon & Schuster, 2000), 45.

11. Richard J. Herrnstein and Charles Murray, *The Bell Curve: Intelligence and Class Structure in American Life* (New York: Free Press, 1994).

12. See Kati Haycock, "Closing the Achievement Gap," *Educational Leadership* 58, no. 6 (March 2001): 6–11.

Chapter 2

The Failure of Reform

For decades, the struggles of urban school systems have preoccupied policy-makers, educators, and others. Mounds of reports, studies, charts, and graphs have attested to the lamentable condition of K–12 education in inner cities and its dire consequences for disadvantaged students. Plentiful have been the speeches from legislature floors, exhortations on editorial pages, and rallies in front of state capitols demanding swift action to end the crisis.

The nation responded with great activity time and time again. The finest minds and strongest backs from successive generations—from perches in government, philanthropy, business, academia, and elsewhere—have tried to redress the inequalities suffered by urban students. As the previous chapter discussed, reformers were not sent into the wilderness without maps. There is a wide body of thought on the underlying causes of the problem, and there has been no shortage of concrete recommendations for change.

In fact, it is striking how well America's reform initiatives have aligned with the leading ideas. Thinkers and practitioners have offered plausible explanations and suggested tightly connected courses of action, with three strategies standing out: increased funding, standards and accountability, and choice and competition. Federal, state, and local leaders have built playbooks from this film study and spared no expense in implementing the game plan.

The only thing more striking than the sensibleness of this work is just how unsuccessful it has been. Despite great investments of mental energy, financial resources, and physical labor, America's urban school districts remain tragically underperforming. In the stark words of one *Harvard Business Review* article, our well-intentioned, relentless efforts "have failed to produce a single high-performing urban school system."[1]

We are then forced to ask how it is possible that so many faithfully executed policies, derived unswervingly from our understanding of the problem, could have come up short repeatedly. After reviewing these initiatives and their continuously discouraging results, it becomes clear that neither our policies nor their implementation is the issue. It's the theories underlying them that have led us astray.

INCREASES IN FUNDING

The most common strategy for improving urban districts in the last several decades has been increases in funding. It's been consistently embraced by the legislative and executive branches of the federal government, state governments, and local governments. When these bodies haven't moved as swiftly or as far as some would have preferred, courts have often forced their hands, requiring substantial increases in financial aid. The result has been a national public school system—especially its urban components—that is remarkably well resourced.

The United States spends more than half a trillion dollars each year on K–12 public education, a figure larger than the GDP of all but sixteen other nations. We also spend more per student than nearly all other developed nations. Funding has grown steadily over the last forty years. In 1965–66, the year the federal Elementary and Secondary Education Act (ESEA) was passed, schools spent $3,883 per pupil in inflation-adjusted dollars (2006–7 constant). As of 2004–5, it had risen to $10,725. After controlling for inflation, per-pupil expenditures increased by more than 25 percent during the previous ten years and more than 60 percent over the previous twenty.

Federal education funds have helped drive these increases, and most of those funds were directed to schools serving low-income students. Controlling for inflation, federal spending on K–12 schooling increased by 275 percent between 1970 and 2005.[2] Title I, the primary federal program for supporting needy schools, has directed nearly $350 billion dollars (constant 2007) to school districts since its inception in 1966.[3] The program was funded at nearly $14 billion in 2008.

Important changes in recent years have greatly expanded the program's reach. Funding levels for Title I grew rapidly in the No Child Left Behind (NCLB) era, increasing by 75 percent from 2000 to 2008.[4] Because of these budget increases and the growth in school-wide Title I programs, the number of students served by Title I ballooned from 6.7 million in 1994–95 to 20.0 million in 2004–5.[5]

Federal aid has been targeted to the lowest-income and lowest-performing schools. Almost 40 percent of federal K–12 funds go to the districts in the highest poverty quartile. This support has grown significantly in recent years: between 1997–98 and 2004–5, the poorest districts saw their number of low-income students grow by only 4 percent while their Title I funds grew by 57 percent. [6]

On average, the federal government provides nearly $1,500 per student to schools in the poorest quartile. Title I funds alone support two extra teachers and one extra teacher aide in the typical Title I school, increasing the number of teachers in these schools by 7 percent and the number of aides by 24 percent.

Since "high-poverty" and "urbanicity" aren't synonymous, it's important to determine whether federal funds are making their way to poor inner-city schools at least at the same rate as to schools in other areas. In fact, urban schools are more likely to receive federal education funding than suburban or rural schools, and they also receive a disproportionate amount of federal funding compared to schools in other locations.

Urban districts have 43 percent of the nation's low-income students yet receive 48 percent of Title I funds; as a result, urban districts receive more than $300 more per poor child than a suburban district. Fully 98 percent of urban districts receive Title I funds, a rate higher than for suburban and rural schools. Urban districts are also more likely to receive funding from Comprehensive School Reform, Title III, and the Perkins program than suburban or rural districts.

These federal streams accomplished precisely what was intended: helping equalize the funding of poor and affluent districts. As of the 2004–5 school year, America's highest-poverty districts had per student revenues virtually equivalent to the nation's lowest-poverty districts ($10,025 to $10,836). State and local funding has also risen significantly. In constant (2007) dollars annual state expenditures on public elementary and secondary education nearly tripled from 1970 to 2005, from about $85 billion to $240 billion. Local funding more than doubled, increasing from $111 billion to $226 billion. [7]

The disproportionate growth in federal and state funding vis-à-vis local funding was purposeful, designed to remedy the inequalities that result when local governments provide the majority of funding. So while all streams have increased, since 1960, federal and state contributions to schools' budgets increased from 4 percent to 9 percent and 39 percent to 47 percent, respectively, while local contributions fell from 57 percent to 44 percent.

Typically, state-level increases resulted from concerns about urban education. The Massachusetts Education Reform Act of 1993 doubled the state's education contributions with greater increases going to struggling districts. An analysis of the law's impact concluded that, "It is obvious that the poorer urban districts have benefited greatly financially."[8] In 2002, the Maryland General Assembly enacted the "Bridge to Excellence in Public Schools Act," largely in response to the struggles of urban districts. The law increased funding by $1.3 billion a year, with Baltimore City and the urban Prince George's County receiving the largest infusions of funds.

In a number of states, city school budgets increased at the direct order of courts or because of the threat of litigation. During the 1970s, two types of school finance cases became popular: "equity" claims charging that urban districts suffered unfair treatment, and "adequacy" claims charging that, irrespective of comparisons with other districts, urban schools had insufficient funds to do their job. Since these cases emerged, more than 125 suits have challenged the spending levels of district and schools.[9]

As of 2005, funding formulas in thirty-six states had been challenged on equity grounds, and a number of these suits proved successful. As a result of the well-known *Abbott* decisions, a number of urban districts in New Jersey are among the highest spending districts in the nation, with expenditures of more than $20,000 per student. In recent years, adequacy suits have proliferated (thirty-nine states had faced adequacy suits by 2006) and generated more wins for plaintiffs.[10] In New York, a 2006 ruling ordered the state to increase funding to New York City by about $5 billion with another $9 billion extra for capital expenditures.

Philanthropies have also contributed. It was estimated that in 2002, foundations and other donors added approximately $1.5 billion to the nation's K–12 education budget.[11] Philanthropic funds are often targeted toward urban areas. The Annenberg Challenge, a $500 billion investment launched in 1993, focused resources on several city school systems, including Boston, Chicago, Detroit, Houston, New York City, and Los Angeles.

These enormous funding increases have had a profound impact on urban districts, including their facilities, programs, administrators, and more. And as funding advocates no doubt desired, the effect on classrooms has been significant.

Student enrollment in public elementary and secondary schools was nearly 46 million in 1970. In that same year there were just over 2 million K–12 public school teachers. By 2005, student enrollment had only increased to 49 million. The number of teachers, however, grew by more than 50 percent to over 3.1 million. As a result, the student-teacher ratio fell dramatically, from 22.3 in 1970 to 15.4 in 2005. Though rural schools have the lowest student-teacher ratios today, the variation between large cities, midsize cities, and the urban fringes of both is only one student per teacher.[12]

During the same period educators gained greater purchasing power. In constant dollars, teacher salaries increased by nearly 10 percent between 1970 and 2005. According to a federal survey, teachers in central cities earned significantly more than rural/small-town teachers and only slightly less than teachers in urban fringe/large towns.[13] Central-city principals earned more than their peers in other geographical locations.[14]

But somehow, despite the massive influx of funds, urban schools continue to poorly educate millions of students. A clear and powerful positive association between money and results just doesn't exist. As one report summarized, "spending increases have outstripped achievement gains, and new funding programs have not propelled students over the performance bars set by states. It seems that the connection between resources has been growing weaker, not stronger."[15]

This finding has been reaffirmed frequently. Scholar Eric Hanushek summarized the research: "Measures of school resources do not provide guidance either about the current quality of schools or about the potential for improving matters." On the efficacy of lawsuits: "The simplest summary is that *no* (emphasis original) currently available evidence shows that past judicial actions about school finance—either related to equity or to adequacy—have had a beneficial effect on student performance."[16]

Data from the National Center for Education Statistics found that in 2005–6 some perennially underachieving city districts spent well above the per-student national average of $9,138, such as New York City ($14,961), Atlanta ($12,345), and Cleveland ($11,073). In fact, some of America's lowest performing urban school districts are also among the nation's highest spending, like Newark, New Jersey ($21,295) and Boston ($17,421). In 2007, the *Washington Post* reported that the nation's capital's school district is "among the highest-spending and worst-performing in the nation."

This mounting evidence against the "drastically increase funding" strategy helped incubate a powerful new argument. Instead of saying that resources didn't matter, some reformers argued for a supportive, parallel strategy based on data showing that, "additional funding for education will not *automatically and necessarily* (emphasis added) generate student achievement."[17]

The standards and accountability movement was this secondary strategy. To many, its primary purpose was to ensure that the nation's ever-expanding education investments were paying dividends.[18] President George W. Bush, during the January 2002 signing ceremony for NCLB—possibly the ultimate expression of the standards and accountability movement—emphasized this theme: "If we've learned anything over the last generations, money alone doesn't make a good school. It certainly helps. But…we've spent billions of dollars with lousy results. So now it's time to spend billions of dollars and get good results."

STANDARDS AND ACCOUNTABILITY

Many posited that for funding increases to make a difference, an additional four-step process was needed. First, schools should know precisely what their students were expected to know in each subject by the end of each grade ("content standards"). Second, schools should have access to instructional guidelines aligned to standards ("curriculum"). Third, there must be tests aligned with standards so we can tell what students had and had not learned ("assessments"). Fourth, if assessment results indicated that students hadn't performed adequately, interventions should be applied to teachers, schools, and districts ("accountability").

This process was meant to bring order and fairness to K–12 education; all interested parties would know in advance what outcomes to expect, and empirical data would reveal the results. More importantly, it was designed to improve learning. With standards providing a clear target at which to aim, schools could carefully direct their attention and resources. With assessments providing unambiguous information about areas of success and failure, educators and policymakers could make needed changes. And with accountability measures providing assistance and pressure, struggling schools would have the resources and incentives to improve.

These policies came about slowly and unevenly among the states. But generally by the 1980s, states were headed in the same direction, catalyzed by several national events. Though a number of studies in the early 1980s, including contributions from the Education Commission of the States and the College Board, argued for elevating expectations and focusing on academic outcomes, none had a greater impact than *A Nation at Risk*. Authored by the National Commission on Excellence in Education, the 1983 report induced the nation to toughen content standards, emphasize mastery of core subjects, increase graduation requirements, and more.

When combined with emerging data indicating declining achievement and warnings from employers that graduates were increasingly unprepared for the workforce, *A Nation at Risk* helped energize a national movement. The report, however, marked more of a change in trajectory than direction.

The nation had gradually become aware of the problem, and districts had begun implementing changes. Between 1980 and 1983, 53 percent of school districts had increased the number of credits required in core subjects. But soon, state governments would take the lead. In particular, a number of governors, like Jim Hunt, Lamar Alexander, Richard Riley, and Bill Clinton, helped push the ascendant standards and accountability movement.

By the early 1980s, thirty-seven states had mandatory competency tests. In 1984, thirty states were working on content standards, curriculum frameworks, or learning outcomes. In 1989, President George H. W. Bush convened all fifty governors to establish performance targets for the nation's schools. The National Council of Teachers of Mathematics published standards for students and teaching in 1989 and 1991, respectively. Meanwhile, states, most notably Texas, North Carolina, and Virginia, continued their efforts to build systems that fully integrated standards, tests, and accountability.

An early success was the 1993 Massachusetts Education Reform Act. It required the state board of education to develop standards and help districts align curriculum and instruction to them. It also led to the development of a statewide assessment and accountability system, which included remedies for persistently low-performing schools. By 1994, sixteen states had full content standards in English, mathematics, science, and social studies.

Through two pieces of legislation in 1994, the federal government advanced the ball. "Goals 2000: The Educate America Act" subsidized state-level efforts to develop standards and assessments, and the "Improving America's Schools Act" (IASA) tied states' eligibility for federal funds to their development of challenging standards and tests. Progress continued through the 1990s. In 1999, Secretary of Education Richard Riley reported that thirty-six states were issuing school report cards. The stage was set for the full realization of the accountability movement.

On January 8, 2002, President George W. Bush signed into law NCLB, which required states to develop standards in key subjects, assess all students in reading and math in grades 3 through 8 and once in high school, intervene in struggling schools, and provide greater choice to students. Though the law had serious implications for all schools, NCLB promised to have the biggest impact on urban systems. It sought to make transparent the staggering underperformance of these schools, provide supports, offer choices to needy students, and strengthen the hand of states dealing with failing districts.

By the 2005–6 school year, all states were administering math and reading assessments. By 2007, half of states had accountability systems that had been approved by the U.S. Department of Education. By the end of the Bush administration in January 2009, thirty-nine states had received approval.

Nevertheless, despite more than two decades of work, America's urban schools are still poorly educating most of their students. Though some proponents point to marginal gains in the performance of city districts and a slight narrowing of the achievement gap, it's become clear that the generation-long move toward standards and accountability simply didn't cause a major sea change in urban districts' performance.

As with the "increased spending" strategy, the failure of standards and accountability to solve our urban school problems can't be simply attributed to poor or unfaithful implementation. City school systems are full participants in the coast-to-coast accountability system. Every urban public school is aware of what its students are expected to learn in basic subjects. The performance of their students is assessed regularly. Those results are made public, and persistent underperformance results in district and state interventions.

And yet the struggles continue. Even in Boston and Houston, two cities whose states have longstanding and well-respected accountability systems, fewer than one in four eighth graders read at the proficient level according to NAEP. Something must be wrong with the theory.

It was thought that all schools—knowing that parents, community members, policymakers, and reporters would have access to their test scores—would improve so as to avoid unwanted attention. This force would be doubly powerful for schools already identified as struggling; having been called out publicly, they would have incentive to improve. With a detailed diagnosis of struggling schools' weaknesses, district and state administrators would be able to intelligently intervene.

But improvement didn't follow identification. For years, state accountability systems had successfully determined which schools were troubled. In a study of five states' school turnaround efforts, the Center for Education Policy found that each state had at least one school that had been marked for improvement for eight years or more.[19] In 2006, when the Maryland State Department of Education sought to take over eleven failing Baltimore schools, it selected schools that had been identified as low-performing since at least 1997.

NCLB only improved states' identification of struggling schools. In the 2005–6 school year, nearly 12,000 schools were tagged for improvement, 84 percent of which were Title I schools. By the 2007–8 school year, nearly thirty thousand schools failed to make adequate yearly progress, and about half of those had missed performance goals for two or more years.

Obviously, identification isn't the problem. Shame and external interventions, the two consequences of identification, had far less impact than expected. Either shame yielded insufficient pressure, fixing urban districts was more difficult than expected, or both. An explanation for shame's muted effects emerges in the following section, and the disappointing results of targeted school improvement efforts, are considered in a later chapter.

CHOICE AND COMPETITION

Some reformers have been as skeptical of accountability as the increased resources strategy. They have argued that city districts suffer from a set of systemic problems resulting from their standing as the dominant, and often only, provider of public schools in a geographic area. Since many urban parents are unable to afford to move to higher-performing school districts or pay for private school tuition, the traditional urban district has a captive consumer base, and therefore the system functions as a monopoly, with no incentive or pressure to improve services, reduce costs, and so on.

Armed with these arguments, some reformers have contended that no amount of funding or external accountability could induce these systems to radically improve. As education scholar Frederick Hess has written, "For those skeptical of district-based reform, the proffered remedy is typically 'parental choice' or 'market competition.'"[20]

Nobel Prize-winning economist Milton Friedman was one of the earliest and strongest advocates of such an approach, arguing it would increase efficiency and performance. Though they haven't been able to implement their vision as fully as the two other sets of reformers, choice and competition advocates have been able to bring about a number of policies that generate the types of forces they think necessary. This is especially true when looking at select cities.

These "choice" and "competition" programs take a number of different forms, but they share a basic characteristic: They expand the options available to families beyond their assigned district public schools by creating new alternatives and/or enabling families to choose from among existing alternatives.

Among the most prominent are those that make private schools more accessible to families. The first such program was created in Milwaukee, Wisconsin, in 1990. In the 2008–9 school year, there were eighteen private school choice programs nationwide (government-supported programs that enable students to attend nonpublic schools) operating in ten states and Washington, D.C. Approximately 171,000 students were participating in these programs. Private school choice initiatives have grown in recent years, with the number of participating students growing by 88 percent over the previous five years.[21]

Generally these programs fall into two categories: first, scholarship or voucher programs, whereby the government provides funding directly to families enabling them to select schools other than their assigned public schools; and second, scholarship tax credit programs, whereby individuals or businesses receive tax credits for contributing to nonprofit organizations that provide scholarships.

Though a number of states have scholarship programs for special education students, most are designed to provide scholarships to low-income students and/or those assigned to failing schools. Examples can be seen in Ohio, Wisconsin, Louisiana, and the District of Columbia. In 2008–9, nearly 62,000 students were participating in government-supported scholarship programs.

Scholarship tax credit programs are also often targeted toward needy students. Programs in Arizona, Florida, Iowa, Pennsylvania, and Rhode Island set family income limits for participating students. Nearly 110,000 students were participating in scholarship tax credit programs in 2008–9.

Charter schools have also expanded the choices available to families, particularly in urban areas. During the 2011–12 school year, there were more than 5,600 charters operating nationwide serving more than 2 million students. Even more importantly for this discussion is the large and growing charter "market share" in many urban communities. According to the National Alliance for Public Charter Schools, in 2010–11, eight communities, including New Orleans, Dayton, Kansas City, and Washington, D.C., had at least 30 percent of their public school students in charter schools.

Generating competitive pressure has been one of the charter world's primary purposes from its inception. A study of the preambles of the nation's state charter school laws found that providing families with more options and spurring competition were among the leading goals of the state legislatures passing charter laws. [22] During his successful campaign for president, Barack Obama argued in favor of charters, saying at one point, "I think it's important to foster competition inside the public schools."

Competition has also been generated by more traditional forms of choice. Many urban districts, including New York City and Boston, allow families to choose from a range of public schools run by the local school system. More than forty states have inter-district choice programs that enable urban students to attend public schools outside of their home districts. [23]

Finally, though its implementation has been hindered by a number of forces, the NCLB public school choice provision requires districts to offer students in struggling schools alternate public schooling options within their borders. In 2006–7, 45,000 students nationwide participated in this program. As a result of these programs, urban school systems have been influenced by the forces of choice and competition for some time, in a number of cases for many years.

However, choice and competition have also had far less impact on the performance of urban districts than many expected. In fact, in a number of cases, choice and competition were vigorously applied to these struggling systems over a number of years, and those districts are as low-performing today as they were before the pressure was applied.

To ascertain the impact of private school vouchers on districts, Hess studied Milwaukee, Cleveland, and Edgewood, Texas, three districts with similar programs. He found that despite the exodus of their students to other schools, little if anything changed in the beleaguered districts. "As it turns out, much of my story is one of nonresponse. In the end, I found myself largely studying why the dog did not bark." [24]

In each of the cities, the district failed to greatly improve student learning or fundamentally alter operations. In Cleveland, even after the voucher program had been in operation for several years, serving nearly four thousand students, "Interviews suggest that neither CPS (Cleveland Public Schools) nor non-CPS observers regarded the voucher program as a serious competitive threat to the CPS. . . . No interviewee could point to any specifics in policy or behavior at the district, school, or classroom level that had been motivated by competition."

After analyzing survey results from Milwaukee, Hess found that, "No more than one in ten teachers interviewed could think of even one substantive effect of competition." Other prominent observers would later concur. Scholar Sol Stern reported "no transformation of the public schools has taken place," and former Milwaukee superintendent and voucher advocate Howard Fuller said, "I think that any honest assessment would have to say that there hasn't been the deep, wholesale improvement in MPS that we would have thought."[25]

A 2008 analysis found eerily similar results in cities facing stiff competition from charters. In Dayton, Ohio, though charters have taken nearly a third of the district's students, the public school system still fails to hit performance benchmarks, and a majority of the public wants major district reform or an entirely new public school system.[26]

In the nation's capital, where one in every three public school students attends a charter school (and another 1,700 attend private schools through the federally funded voucher program), the district appears impervious: District of Columbia Public Schools (DCPS) remains among the very lowest performing districts in the nation according to NAEP. As a 2005 study of Washington, D.C.,'s charter sector concluded: "Thus far, there is no clear evidence that charter schools have had a direct impact on student achievement in DCPS schools or otherwise driven systemic reform."[27]

The results are similar in city after city. A study of Michigan reported, "Overall there is little evidence of fundamental changes in teaching and learning or of significant improvement in student achievement in the districts most affected by charter schools."[28] Detroit's district has lost nearly 30 percent of its students to charters, but nonetheless has the nation's lowest graduation rate.

Though Hess's study of Cleveland ended in 2000, another decade of competition, including the continuation of the voucher program and a charter sector with 22 percent market share, did little to improve the district. In the 2007 NAEP Trial Urban District Assessment, Cleveland eighth graders scored lower in math and reading than the students in every other city participating, including notorious low performers such as Washington, D.C., Atlanta, and Chicago. A 2009 *Cleveland Plain Dealer* article titled "Cleveland's Battered Schools" noted that thirty years earlier the paper had written an article with the very same themes.

Scholars have produced a significant body of rigorous empirical research in this area.[29] A leading choice scholar, Stanford's Caroline Hoxby, has studied how public schools respond when surrounded by a large number of private schools or public school districts or when facing voucher or charter competition. Generally, she has found statistically significant but relatively small improvements in the affected public schools.

The University of Arkansas' Jay Greene, another prominent choice scholar, also found small but statistically significant benefits in public school performance attributable to voucher competition.[30] Similarly Greene and Ryan Marsh, studying Milwaukee's program, reported that affected public schools were lifted modestly by competition's rising tide, "but that tide has not exactly been a tsunami."[31] Scholar Marcus Winters found charters had quite small positive competitive effects in New York City.[32]

A number of other researchers have studied this issue through different approaches, and their conclusions have been inconsistent, some finding competitive benefits, others not.[33] But even the most sanguine results only suggest that competition has a marginal positive influence on student achievement or impact on system behavior; none make the case that competition has brought about a sea change. Certainly, no study has substantiated the confident claim that competition would be a "panacea" for improving districts.

After considering these research findings alongside the continued poor performance of numerous urban districts despite the introduction of choice and competition, the fairest conclusion is that competition, as currently understood in K–12 education, wasn't the cure for the failings of inner-city school systems.

Consequently some choice advocates have recently expressed disillusionment with the powers of competition. Stern, a voucher supporter, has written about his search for a "Plan B" for students not receiving vouchers because of the "meager" evidence that competition improves districts. Former Reagan-administration Assistant Education Secretary Chester E. Finn, Jr., expressed "growing sympathy" with those expressing skepticism of educational competition and warned of placing "too much trust in market forces."[34]

But this concern and cynicism is misguided. Given the indisputable benefits of competition in other fields, these findings should force us to look askance at urban school districts, not competition. If a newly discovered plant species doesn't grow when exposed to sunlight and water, we don't begin doubting photosynthesis; we investigate what about this particular plant makes these proven interventions unsuccessful in this specific case.

Looking further into the relationship between urban education and competition, we quickly see that their incompatibility is attributable to the characteristics of the former, not the deficiencies of the latter.

SO WHAT WENT WRONG?

Given that increased resources, accountability, and competition have succeeded in other fields, it should give us pause that they've failed to bring about major improvements in urban districts. How is this possible?

It is because these forces, though powerful, are not omnipotent. They cannot—either individually or in concert—bring about optimal results on their own. The success of each depends on a well-functioning system. That is, their influence will be enlarged or muted by other dynamics.

This is true elsewhere. Even pervasive, potent forces like democracy and capitalism require other systemic elements to work. If a nation lacks freedom of speech, an independent press, and civilian control of the military, then democratic elections will likely mean little. If a nation lacks a common currency, property rights, and contract enforcement, then free and flourishing markets can't truly emerge.

The same lesson applies to urban public schooling. As the rest of this book will argue, it suffers from a deep system problem, best thought of as a "portfolio" problem. The traditional urban district has dreadfully managed its collection of schools to the detriment of the entire system. Districts have been loath to close persistently failing schools. They have generally been unwilling to regularly create new and diverse offerings—and they've been even more unwilling to have others operate new schools. They have not regularly replicated and expanded their best schools.

By causing the portfolio of schools to remain virtually unchanged from year to year, these practices have directly prevented the aggregate quality of the city's collection of schools from improving over time. But it has also reduced the positive effects of forces like accountability and competition.

In other industries, transparent performance metrics and consumers' ability to choose from an array of options contribute to system-wide improvement because there are consequences for continued poor performance. A low-quality firm will be forced to fold, creating a powerful incentive for self-improvement. Similarly, a record of exceptionally high performance in other fields will lead an organization to expand, providing another incentive for quality.

In urban districts, however, the consequence of persistent failure (for adults) has been insignificant. As one set of scholars wrote, the upshot of failure has never been "existence-threatening" for schools.[35] In the words of a U.S. Department of Education report, "Businesses operate under the immediate threat of bankruptcy and termination; schools typically do not."[36] Similarly, a school's continuous remarkable success has had practically no organizational consequences for the school itself or systemic consequences for the district.

The pages to come will further explain and build on these points, namely that properly managing a city's portfolio of schools is essential to high-performance and continuous improvement. As importantly, and more provocatively, they will argue that the traditional district structure is incapable of leading this process and must be replaced.

Chapter 6 discusses the invaluable role such "portfolio management" plays in the health of other industries and identifies how this can be accomplished within public education. Chapter 5 explains why the district is poorly suited to lead this work. Chapter 4 recounts the district's consistent mismanagement of a key element of portfolio management, addressing failing schools.

But first, the following chapter will reveal the nature of school quality within the district portfolio, suggesting why it needs to be carefully managed and laying the groundwork for why the three sectors of schools ought to be integrated into a coherent, comprehensive urban school system.

NOTES

1. Stacey Childress, Richard Elmore, and Allen Grossman, "How to Manage Urban School Districts," *Harvard Business Review*, November 2006, 55.

2. See Table 32 in Thomas D. Snyder, Sally A. Dillow, and Charlene M. Hoffman, *Digest of Education Statistics 2007* (Washington, DC: National Center for Education Statistics, Institute for Education Sciences, U.S. Department of Education, 2008), http://nces.ed.gov/pubs2008/2008022.pdf.

3. U.S. Department of Education, *National Assessment of Title I: Final Report, Summary of Key Findings*, October 2007, Exhibit B-2, 156.

4. "Improving Basic Programs Operated by Local Educational Agencies (Title I, Part A)—Funding Status," U.S. Department of Education, last modified August 31, 2011, http://www2.ed.gov/programs/titleiparta/funding.html.

5. U.S. Department of Education, *National Assessment of Title I: Final Report*, 6.

6. Jay G. Chambers, et al., *State and Local Implementation of the No Child Left Behind Act: Volume VI—Targeting and Uses of Federal Education Funds* (Jessup, MD: Education Publications Center, U.S. Department of Education, 2009), 38, http://www2.ed.gov/rschstat/eval/disadv/nclb-targeting/nclb-targeting.pdf.

7. Table 32 in Snyder, Dillow, and Hoffman, *Digest of Education Statistics 2007.*

8. Linda Driscoll, et al., "Education Reform: Ten Years after the Massachusetts Education Reform Act of 1993," *Education Connections* (Amherst: University of Massachusetts Amherst School of Education, 2003), http://npe.educationnews.org/Review/Resources/ed.connection.2003.pdf.

9. James W. Guthrie and Matthew G. Springer, "Courtroom Alchemy," *EducationNext*7, no. 1, (Winter 2007), 21.

10. See Martin R. West and Paul E. Peterson, "The Adequacy Lawsuit: A Critical Apprai-sal," in *School Money Trials: The Legal Pursuit of Educational Adequacy*, eds. Martin R. West and Paul E. Peterson (Washington, DC: Brookings Institution Press, 2007), 6.

11. Jay Greene, "Buckets into the Sea: Why Philanthropy Isn't Changing Schools, and How It Could" (presented at American Enterprise Institute conference "With the Best of Intentions: Lessons Learned in K–12 Education Philanthropy," Washington, DC, April 25, 2005).

12. See Table 12 in Gregory A. Strizek, et al., *Characteristics of Schools, Districts, Teach-ers, Principals, and School Libraries in the United States: 2003–04 Schools and Staffing Survey (NCES 2006-313 Revised)*. U.S. Department of Education, National Center for Educa-tion Statistics (Washington, DC: U.S. Government Printing Office, 2007).

13. See Table 24 in. Strizek, et al., *Characteristics of Schools, Districts, Teachers, Princi-pals, and School Libraries in the United States*.

14. See Table 30 in Strizek, et al., *Characteristics of Schools, Districts, Teachers, Princi-pals, and School Libraries in the United States*.

15. See "Message from the Chair," in Jacob E. Adams, Jr., *Funding Student Learning: How to Align Education Resources with Student Learning Goals*, National Working Group on Fund-ing Student Learning, (Bothell: Center on Reinventing Public Education, University of Wash-ington Bothell, 2008), 7–10.

16. Eric A. Hanushek, "Good Intentions Captured: School Funding Adequacy and the Courts," in *Courting Failure: How School Finance Lawsuits Exploit Judges' Good Intentions and Harm Our Children*, ed. Eric A. Hanushek (Stanford, CA: EducationNext Books, 2006), xiii–xxxii.

17. *Making Money Matter*, Helen Ladel and Janet S. Hansen, editors, Commission on Behavioral and Social Sciences and Education, National Research Council (1999), Washing-ton, DC, National Academy Press, p. 267.

18. "The standards and accountability movement is the result of decades of confusion and disappointment about how resources translate into student outcomes." In Hanushek, "Good Intentions Captured."

19. Caitlin Scott, *A Call to Restructure Restructuring: Lessons from the No Child Left Behind Act in Five States*, (Washington, DC: Center on Education Policy, 2008), 9.

20. Frederick M. Hess, "The Supply Side of School Reform," *Phi Delta Kappan* 90, no. 3 (November 2008), 211–17.

21. Geoffrey Goodman, et al., *School Choice Yearbook, 2008–9* (Washington, DC: Alli-ance for School Choice, 2009), http://www.clikproductions.com/PDFs/Year-book_02062009_finalWEB.pdf.

22. Andy Smarick, *Original Intent: What Legislative History Tells Us about The Purposes of Chartering* (Washington, DC: National Alliance for Public Charter Schools, 2005).

23. Erin Dillon, *Plotting School Choice: The Challenge of Crossing District Lines* (Wash-ington, DC: Education Sector, August 2008), 1, http://www.educationsector.org/sites/default/files/publications/Interdistrict_Choice.pdf.

24. Frederick M. Hess, *Revolution at the Margins: The Impact of Competition on Urban School System* (Washington, DC: Brookings Institution Press, 2003).

25. Cited in Frederick M. Hess, "After Milwaukee," *The American*, September/October 2008, 50–2.

26. See Andy Smarick, "Wave of the Future," *EducationNext* 8, no. 1 (Winter 2008), 42–3.

27. Sara Mead, *Capital Campaign: Early Returns on District of Columbia Charter Schools* (Washington, DC: Progressive Policy Institute, October 2005), 18.

28. Sara Mead, *Maintenance Required: Charter Schooling in Michigan* (Washington, DC: Education Sector, October 2006), 14.

29. See Caroline M. Hoxby, *Do Private Schools Provide Competition for Public Schools?*, Working Paper 4978 (Cambridge, MA: National Bureau of Economic Research, 1994); Caro-line M. Hoxby, "Analyzing School Choice Reforms That Use America's Traditional Forms of Parental Choice," in *Learning from School Choice*, eds. Paul E. Peterson and Bryan C. Hassel (Washington, DC: Brookings, 1998), 133–154; Caroline M. Hoxby, "Does Competition among Public Schools Benefit Students and Taxpayers?" *American Economic Review* 90 (2000): 1209–38; "School Choice and School Productivity (Or, Could School Choice Be a Tide That

Lifts All Boats?),” Working Paper 8873 (Cambridge, MA: National Bureau of Economic Research, 2001); Caroline Minter Hoxby, “Rising Tide,” *EducationNext* 1, no. 4 (Winter 2001).

30. Jay Greene, *An Evaluation of the Florida A-Plus Accountability and School Choice Program*, Civic Report (New York: Manhattan Institute for Policy Research, 2001).

31. Patrick Wolf, *The Comprehensive Longitudinal Evaluation of the Milwaukee Parental Choice Program: Summary of Second Year Reports*, SCDP Milwaukee Evaluation (Fayetteville, AR: School Choice Demonstration Project, March 2009).

32. Marcus Winters, *Everyone Wins: How Charter Schools Benefit All New York City Public School Students*, Civic Report (New York: Manhattan Institute for Policy Research, October 2009).

33. See Melvin V. Borland and Roy M. Howsen, “Student Academic Achievement and the Degree of Market Concentration in Education,” *Economics of Education Review* 11, no. 1 (1992): 31–39; Thomas S. Dee, “Competition and the Quality of Public Schools,” *Economics of Education Review* 17, no. 4 (1998): 419–27; Christopher Jepsen, “The Effects of Private School Competition on Student Achievement,” Working Paper 99-16 (Evanston, IL: Institute for Policy Research, Northwestern University, 1999), http://www.ipr.northwestern.edu/publications/papers/jepsenwp99.pdf ; Kevin B. Smith and Kenneth J. Meier, *The Case Against School Choice: Politics, Markets, and Fools* (Armonk, NY: M.E. Sharpe, 1995); Amy Stuart Wells, et al., *Beyond the Rhetoric of Charter School Reform: A Study of Ten California School Districts* (Los Angeles: UCLA Charter School Study, 1998); Paul Teske, et al., “Can Charter Schools Change Traditional Public Schools?,” in *Charter Schools, Vouchers, and Public Education*, eds. Paul E Peterson and David Campbell (Washington, DC: Brookings Institution, 2001); George M. Holmes, Jeff DeSimone, and Nicholas G. Rupp, “Friendly Competition,” *EducationNext* 6, no. 1 (Winter 2006); Robert Bifulco and Helen F. Ladd, “Results from the Tar Heel State,” *EducationNext* 5, no. 4 (Fall 2005).

34. As quoted in Elizabeth Green, “A Libertarian Is Searching For an Education ‘Plan B,’” *New York Sun*, January 14, 2008.

35. Kieran Walshe, et al., “Organizational Failure and Turnaround: Lessons for Public Services from the For-Profit Sector,” *Public Money & Management* 24, no. 4 (August 2004): 201–208.

36. Rebecca Herman, et al., *Turning Around Chronically Low-Performing Schools: A Practice Guide*. NCEE #2008-4020. (Washington, DC: National Center for Education Evaluation and Regional Assistance, Institute of Education Sciences, U.S. Department of Education, 2008), 1, http://ies.ed.gov/ncee/wwc/publications/practiceguides.

Chapter 3

The Quality Curve

The preceding chapters painted a distressing picture of urban public education: school systems with tragically low performance seemingly unaffected by decades of reforms. But every forest is made up of many individual trees. It might not be the case that the general characteristics of this entire sector apply to each school. In fact, we may expect some level of variation within each district. Perhaps only the very-lowest-income schools are truly struggling, and since their stories are so heartbreaking, they color our perspective and the aggregate numbers. Maybe those schools with more economic diversity do better but succeed in silence.

We have reason to suspect some variation. There are famous examples of astonishingly strong principals and teachers succeeding in challenging neighborhoods. Jaime Escalante, dubbed the "best teacher in America" and subject of the film *Stand and Deliver*, annually helped dozens of students pass the Advanced Placement calculus exam in Los Angeles's very poor Garfield High.

It's not uncommon to find an article in a city newspaper telling the story of an urban school beating the odds. Annually, the U.S. Department of Education awards "blue ribbons" to outstanding schools, and each year a number of urban public schools are honored. In 2000, the book *No Excuses* shined a light on twenty-one highly effective low-income schools including fourteen traditional urban public schools. The Education Trust's report *Dispelling the Myth* identified 366 "top performing high poverty schools" from across the country. In 2007, Karin Chenoweth's *It's Being Done* told the story of numerous high-performing, high-poverty schools. [1]

Are these successful schools merely anomalous, isolated cases, or do they speak to a larger phenomenon? What does the actual distribution of quality among urban public schools look like?

27

DATA

To begin the study, the largest American school district was selected. New York City Public Schools educates over one million students. Since elementary schools comprise the bulk of district schools, these were selected for the primary analysis. A scatterplot was created showing each school's poverty rate (free or reduced-price lunch level or "FRPL") and proficiency score on the state's reading and math assessment (Figures 3.1 and 3.2).

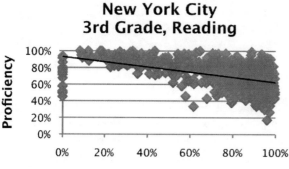

Figure 3.1

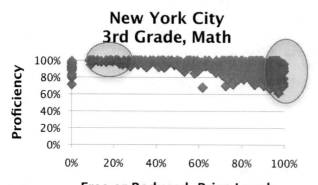

Figure 3.2

Several fascinating results emerge. First, the well-known negative correlation between poverty and performance is immediately revealed. The average proficiency score of schools with the lowest levels of poverty is considerably higher than the average score of the poorest schools. The "best-fit" line added to the reading scores indicates that, on average, a 10-percentage point increase in FRPL level equals a 3-percentage point decrease in proficiency.

But, second, and of great importance, both graphs clearly demonstrate heteroskedasticity, meaning that there is much greater variance among observations at one end of the scale. So while the more affluent schools have consistent high achievement scores (indicated by the thin horizontal oval over schools in the upper left of the Figure 3.2), the very poor schools have widely varying achievement levels (indicated by the long vertical oval on the right). So among New York City's poorest schools, income is far from deterministic; something else is occurring within these schools to enable some to thrive.

To ensure that these findings aren't unique to New York City or third grade, another district and another primary grade is tested. Los Angeles has the nation's second largest district. Math and reading scores from fourth grade were investigated.

The pattern holds: a negative relationship between poverty and achievement but enormous variation in quality among the poorest schools. For example, in two nearly identical low-income schools (both with more than 95 percent of students qualifying for FRPL), there is a 64-percentage point difference in student proficiency on the state's math test (Figure 3.3). Among schools with 10 percent FRPL or less the largest variation is 14 percentage points; among schools with 20 percent FRPL or less, it is 28 points. In reading, two schools with 80 percent FRPL differ in proficiency by 65 points.

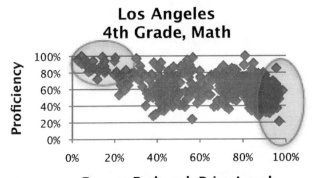

Figure 3.3

Remarkably, the same pattern emerges in four other large districts: Baltimore, Detroit, Houston, and Milwaukee. It is apparent in reading *and* math in third *and* fourth grades (Figure 3.4). These results are also found in secondary schools. Said simply, you can trust that higher income schools will have very high percentages of students passing the state's assessments, but there will be enormous variation in the performance of the lowest income schools.

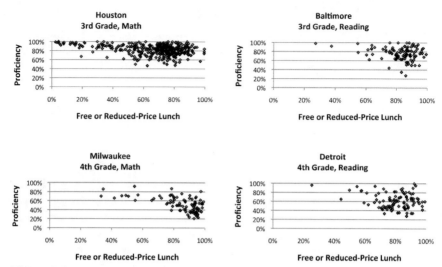

Figure 3.4

These similarities are all the more remarkable because though each district is "large," "urban," and mostly poor, they are different in nontrivial ways. Geographically they represent the Northeast, the Mid-Atlantic, the upper Midwest, the Sun Belt, and the West. Baltimore, Detroit, and Milwaukee have been losing population for years, while Los Angeles and Houston have been growing. New York City, Los Angeles, and Houston are three of the nation's largest cities, while Baltimore and Milwaukee are mid-sized.

New York City Public Schools closely mirrors the racial composition of the average major urban school district.[2] Los Angeles and Houston schools are overwhelmingly Hispanic, while Baltimore and Detroit schools are over-whelmingly African American.

The phenomenon becomes even more interesting when depicted in histograms. Since it appears that quality variation—especially large drop-offs in performance—begin when schools reach 60 percent FRPL, only schools above that figure are considered. In city after city and in grade after grade the results are the same: a remarkably broad distribution. While the theory of statistics prepares us for a bell-shaped, "normal" distribution, the breadth of the variation is staggering.

Milwaukee's and Detroit's schools illustrate this pattern well (Figure 3.5). Among this set of very poor Milwaukee schools, though the average third grade math proficiency rate is only 42 percent, the standard deviation is 18 percentage points, meaning the mean performance rate reveals little about the entire set because the average school has a score nearly 20 points away.

Fourteen schools scored above 60 percent, including one school with 97 percent poverty. In the highest-performing low-income school (with 86 percent proficiency), more than two-thirds of students qualify for subsidized lunches. On the other end of the spectrum, nine schools had proficiency rates under 20 percent, with the lowest at 3 percent. Similarly, in Detroit the gap between the highest and lowest performing schools in third grade reading is more than 70 points; the standard deviation is more than 16 points. One school reaching 100 percent proficiency has a poverty rate of 92 percent.

Milwaukee (Schools > 60% FRPL) 3rd Grade, Math

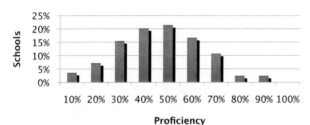

Figure 3.5a

Detroit (Schools > 60% FRPL) 3rd Grade, Math

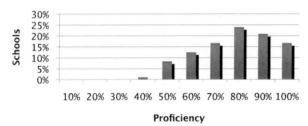

Figure 3.5b

In Los Angeles (Figure 3.6), the average school fourth grade reading proficiency rate is about 50 percent, but the scores range from 20 percent to 93 percent. In fact, 10 percent of schools have proficiency rates above 70 or below 30.

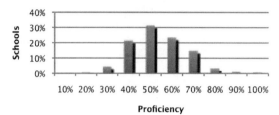

Figure 3.6a

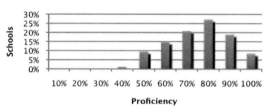

Figure 3.6b

These findings hold in higher grades (Figure 3.7). New York City's average eighth grade reading proficiency ranges from 100 percent to 9 percent. The highest- and lowest-performing schools differ in poverty rates by fewer than 7 percentage points.

It is critical to bear in mind, however, that the relative position of each curve along the x-axis (how far to the left or right) has limited meaning, especially for comparing one city's results to another. Since each state has a different accountability system, were the schools in one city to move to another, their curve would shift, in some cases to a substantial degree.[3] But what remains consistent is the astonishing breadth of variation in performance among low-income schools.

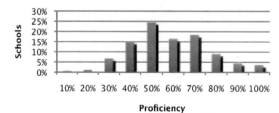

Figure 3.7a

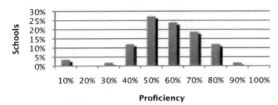

Figure 3.7b

In fact, for the only instances where scores don't take on the full bell-curve shape, it's because the right side was truncated by a state's low proficiency bar (Figure 3.8). In these examples, significant percentages of schools had 100 percent proficiency. Had the assessment been more difficult or the cut score for proficiency been raised, a right side of the distribution almost certainly would appear.

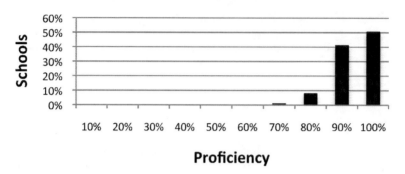

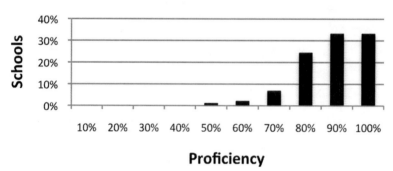

Figure 3.8

Regarding Houston's roseate scores in Figure 3.8, a 2007 study reported, "Texas's tests are below average in terms of difficulty" and found that its third grade cut scores, especially in reading, were set lower than other states.[4] The 2007 NAEP Trial Urban District Assessment in reading found that only 17 percent of the city's fourth graders and 18 percent of its eighth graders reached proficiency.[5]

While Baltimore's and New York City's math results show large percentages of schools with perfect or near-perfect proficiency rates, the 2009 NAEP TUDA found that only 13 percent and 35 percent of students in these cities, respectively, reached proficiency. These facts call into question the east-west placement of these curves but not the distribution. This shape that reappears time and time again regardless of grade or subject is the key finding. It should hold our attention and raise challenging new questions.

Although the link between school wealth and school performance has been known for years, the conventional wisdom—that the poorer a school, the worse its performance (Figure 3.9)—is incomplete. While income is a startlingly strong predictor of school achievement at low levels of poverty (those schools will do very well), its predictive power all but disappears at the highest levels of poverty (Figure 3.10). In urban areas, school performance falls not along a line, but within a right triangle.

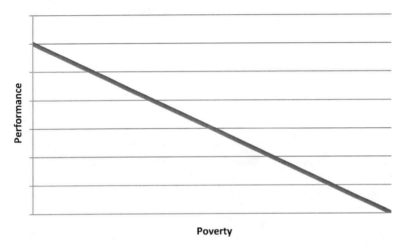

Figure 3.9 Conventional Wisdom: School Wealth and School Performance

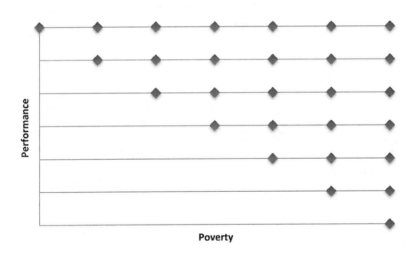

Figure 3.10 High-Poverty Schools and School Performance

This relates directly to another broadly held notion of urban education—that only occasionally will a high-performing high-poverty school emerge. These data paint a different picture. Such schools are far from anomalous. They appear with impressive regularity. They exist in every city at multiple grade levels and in multiple subjects. Their ranks include schools with poverty rates of 60 percent, 70 percent, 80 percent, 90 percent, and more.

These schools aren't curious outliers—distant, unconnected outposts (Figure 3.11). They are the right tail of a broad distribution of quality (Figure 3.12). Just behind them are a significant number of schools outperforming the district's average.

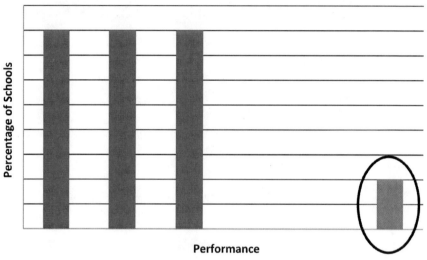

Figure 3.11

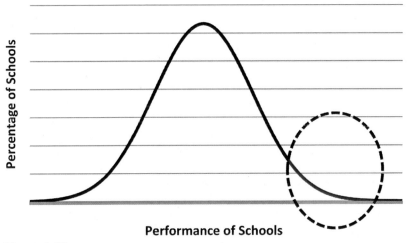

Figure 3.12

Finally, this fact raises a much larger issue. This normal distribution has been shown to apply to everything from statistical error terms to human heights to major league batting averages. If that's the case, the implications are profound. If urban public schooling's quality variation is common, why as a whole has the field produced such staggeringly poor results over time? That is, how can the medical profession or the technology industry have a broad distribution of quality at any given moment but still achieve powerful results and continuously improve over time while urban education's curve is mired mostly in underperformance?

The answer, alluded to earlier, is that these districts have not done what's necessary to move the distribution to the right. Whereas other industries have developed similar practices for generating continuous improvement, urban districts have been unique in their reliance on failed strategies and disregard for successful ones. Said another way, other fields properly manage their portfolios, and urban districts do not. The next chapter begins to detail the nature of this problem and suggest solutions, a process that is more fully developed in chapter 6 and completed in chapter 12.

But understanding the challenge and building a response begins with the distribution itself. First, what do we make of those schools on the right-hand side? What do thriving industries do with their highest performers? Second, while the curves represent today's schools portfolio, do they necessarily represent tomorrow's? Can new schools get added to the mix—and should they? How do other fields think about changes in their portfolios?

Third, although in the graphics above schools are represented as identical dots and invisible components of columns, there are significant differences among them. Isn't diversity an important part of a portfolio? Might not a student have a better chance at success in one type of school than in another?

Finally, what do we do about all of those left-side—low-performing—schools? These are our most pressing problem because they are endangering the educational future of countless students. What's the proper way to address these failing institutions?

These seemingly disparate questions are actually intimately related. In one sense, that is fortunate, because the right strategy might address them all. In another, it poses a challenge because untangling the brush and finding a point of entry is difficult. However, the fourth set of questions offers the best opening. Were we to accomplish nothing else, even moderately improving the chances of students assigned to failing schools would be a victory. It is also the area that has received the most attention for years. Prior attempts to fix these failing schools are too numerous to count, and they provide invaluable lessons.

Finally, and most importantly, studying previous efforts reveals the deeply flawed principles undergirding the district system and explains why other practices essential to an industry's continuous improvement were never adopted. Accordingly, chapter 4 addresses our failed strategy for addressing left-side schools.

NOTES

1. See Samuel Casey Carter, *No Excuses: Lessons from 21 High-Performing, High-Poverty Schools* (Washington, DC: Heritage Foundation, 2000); Patte Barth, et al., eds., *Dispelling the Myth: High Poverty Schools Exceeding Expectations* (Washington, DC: Education Trust, 1999); Karin Chenoweth, *"It's Being Done": Academic Success in Unexpected Schools* (Boston: Harvard Education Press, 2007).

2. Comparative data available via Urban School Statistics, Council of Great City Schools, http://www.cgcs.org/site/default.aspx?pageid=75.

3. According to a 2009 report, of eighteen schools studied, seventeen would have made Adequate Yearly Progress if located in Wisconsin, but if located in Massachusetts, only one would have made AYP. Yun Xiang, John Cronin, and Michael Dahlin, *The Accountability Illusion* (Washington, DC: Thomas B. Fordham Institute, February 2009).

4. John Cronin, et al., *The Proficiency Illusion* (Washington, DC: Thomas B. Fordham Institute, October 2007).

5. *The Nation's Report Card: Trial Urban District Snapshot Report, Reading 2007* (Washington, DC: Institute of Education Sciences, U.S. Department of Education, 2007).

Chapter 4

The Failure of Fixing

The previous chapter laid the foundation for this book's central argument: that properly managing a city's portfolio of schools is essential to creating a healthy urban education system. This chapter builds on this idea, discussing the necessity of properly addressing the lowest-performing schools.

Outside of urban public education, it is difficult to find a field that so comprehensively, consistently, and expensively produces such distressing results. While other industries seem to excel, innovating and improving quality while simultaneously navigating changing consumer demands and resource challenges, urban districts appear mired in perpetual poor performance.

But all fields have individual failures. Some car dealerships have surly staffs, and some carpenters build lousy decks. Countless promising start-ups prove unable to generate profits. Longstanding nonprofits occasionally deteriorate. Even once-mighty corporate giants are susceptible to precipitous decline.

The central contention of this chapter is that what makes urban districts unique is that their failures continue on. Elsewhere, persistent lowest performers go away. They are liquidated, or taken over, fired or reassigned. They go out of business. They file for bankruptcy. But not in urban K–12 education. The worst schools often go on forever. This has obvious and tragic implications for the students assigned to them. But what has been insufficiently recognized is that stubbornly maintaining failing schools has dire consequences for the system as a whole.

WHY DO FAILING SCHOOLS SURVIVE?

Low-performing schools generally exist in perpetuity because of the nature of districts. The first factor is the historical role of geography in school assignments. For ages, the public school a student attended was determined by his home address. Each school was given a residential zone, and every child seeking a public education living within those borders attended that school.

In this context, it's clear why many assumed that each school ought to go on forever: If a neighborhood had children, it needed a school. Thus the school's lifespan was determined by the existence of neighborhood kids, not its quality. To the extent a closure was considered, several additional factors would've weighed against it. Not only would the affected students be displaced, they would have to attend another community's school, causing transportation challenges, possible overcrowding, and more. Closure would have also jeopardized jobs.

Finally, had a neighborhood's school been deemed underperforming, the immediate reaction would have been simple: Improve it! Replace the principal. Increase the budget. Vote out the school board. Change superintendents. There was no reason to believe that a school's weaknesses couldn't be addressed. The possibility of continuous school failure rooted in systemic dysfunction wasn't part of the discussion when the concept of public school immortality was born.

Today, a number of these factors seem like relics of a bygone era. We now know that assignments need not be based on geography and that schools can be replaced. We know that choice and public education are compatible. We also know that replacing old textbooks or recalcitrant board members doesn't necessarily improve a school's performance.

But even if schools don't *have* to exist forever, why not behave as though they should? One could argue that preserving them maintains continuity, protects jobs, and demonstrates our unwillingness to give up. Perhaps ongoing improvement efforts have personal, community, and symbolic value.

Unfortunately, efforts to fix long-broken schools simply don't work like we need them to. The evidence shows forcefully that turning around failing schools is not a scalable strategy for improving urban systems. Moreover, by putting so much of our energy into preserving failing schools, we have actually impeded the development of other activities central to the healthy management of our portfolio of schools.

YESTERDAY'S AND TODAY'S SCHOOLS

Education scholar Ted Kolderie argues that our inability to drastically improve K–12 education is attributable to our fidelity to yesterday's schools. Rather than embracing the regular creation of new schools, "The discussion has been almost entirely about getting the better by transforming the existing."[1] As he and colleague Joe Graba have written, "We cannot get the schools we need by changing the schools we have."[2]

Their thinking builds upon the research of acclaimed business professor Clayton Christensen. Christensen and colleagues have found that in the private sector, existing organizations are seldom able to change themselves sufficiently to address the new realities caused by "disruptive innovations." Because these older organizations have longstanding practices and beliefs geared toward yesterday's conditions, they are unable to adapt. The new landscape will be controlled by new entrants or, if an existing organization hopes to survive, wholly independent subsidiaries.[3]

Applying this logic to K–12 schooling leads to a jarring hypothesis: School turnarounds, school restructurings, and the like are destined to fail. Fortunately, we can test the hypothesis. Thanks to the decades-old accountability movement, culminating in the federal No Child Left Behind (NCLB) Act, we have an understanding of which schools are failing and thousands of examples of intervention strategies. Based on all of this work, what have we learned about turnarounds?

THE STICKINESS OF FAILURE

As a rule, virtually all low-performing schools remain low-performing. As one research institute concluded, "Efforts to turn chronically failing schools around have largely failed."[4] Salient examples abound: in the first year of California's Academic Performance Index, the lowest-performing 20 percent of schools were identified. After interventions, of the 968 elementary schools in this category, only 11 percent were able to make "exemplary progress." More distressingly, only one of the 394 middle and high schools in this category made such progress.[5]

In 2008, fifty-two Ohio schools were forced to restructure because of persistent failure. They made little if any progress. Fewer than one in three were even able to reach a higher number of academic goals, and fewer than one in two showed any gains in student performance. The *Columbus Dispatch* concluded, "few of them have improved significantly even after years of effort and millions in tax dollars." A union leader agreed, "This hasn't worked. I have seen that students are worse off than they were before."[6]

Two astounding 2010 studies powerfully confirmed what these anecdotes suggested. A report from the Brookings Institution found that of the California schools in the lowest-performing quartile in 1989, only 1.4 percent were in the highest-performing quartile twenty years later.[7]

Similarly, researcher David Stuit tracked more than two thousand low-performing schools from across the nation for five years. Fewer than one in ten were able to rise from the lowest-performing quartile to the second-lowest-performing quartile. Worse, only 1 percent were able to rise from the lowest-performing quartile to the top half of performance.[8]

DEFINING TURNAROUND DOWN

Somehow this body of research has yet to influence thinking in the education world. One reason is that what constitutes a successful improvement effort has become muddled. Advocates can debate how low-performing a school needs to be and how long it needs to struggle in order to be turnaround-eligible.[9] There are differences of opinion on how long the turnaround process can take. There's no consensus on how drastic the improvement needs to be or long how it must be sustained.

As a result, some have offered hazy definitions for success or merely defined success down.[10] One group defines a turnaround as "any strategy intended to significantly improve academic outcomes for substantially the same group of students within two years."[11] Another says success generates "substantial gains in student learning in year one that were then sustained over time."[12] A third says it produces significant achievement gains within two years followed by a longer period of sustained improvement.[13]

The U.S. Department of Education report, "Turning Around Chronically Low-Performing Schools," sets the bar strikingly low: A successful turnaround is a school with at least 20 percent of students failing to meet academic standards for at least two years that lowers failure rates or improves proficiency rates by 10 percentage points within three years.

Such indeterminateness has caused many to fall back on intuition or hope—that rapid improvement is not only possible but also common. It has also allowed some debatable strategies to gain a reputation for success. One heralded program has reported good but far from spectacular results: about half of its targeted schools have either made AYP or reduced math and reading failure rates by at least 5 percent.[14]

NCLB AND FAILING SCHOOLS

NCLB, however, brought some order to this discussion. Since the law required states to establish benchmarks for schools and track progress, we can identify the number of schools failing to lift achievement above performance floors and determine how long those schools remain under-performing.

The U.S. Department of Education identified all schools in "improvement status" in 2004–5, and then tracked their status two years later. In order to exit improvement status, these schools merely had to make AYP both years. Yet only 28 percent were able to do so.[15] These schools only had to lift performance above a low floor, not reach exemplary achievement levels. And they only had to sustain this meager progress for two years. Even with the bar set so low, fewer than three in ten were successful.

Even more alarming was the success rate of schools in NCLB-mandated restructuring, those with five or more consecutive years of underperformance. Only 19 percent of these schools were able to exit improvement status two years later.

The 2008 Center on Education Policy study, "A Call to Restructure Restructuring," found even more troubling results. In California, Maryland, and Ohio, only 14 percent, 12 percent, and 9 percent of schools in restructuring, respectively, made AYP the following year, so the percentage of schools making AYP two consecutive years (the criteria considered for "success rates" above) would be even lower.

Moreover, we must consider whether making AYP constitutes success: In 2009, a California school could meet its target if slightly more than a third of its students reached proficiency.[16] The success rates in Michigan and Georgia were higher, but these must be judged skeptically. Michigan changed its accountability system during this period, and both states set their bars especially low.[17] A 2009 analysis found that both have "relatively easy" proficiency standards compared to other states and use other techniques that increase the ability of schools to reach targets. That analysis found that while only one elementary school of a sample of eighteen would have made AYP in Massachusetts, seven would have in Georgia and ten in Michigan.[18]

OWNING UP TO FAILED IMPROVEMENT EFFORTS

The consequences of our misguided devotion to turnarounds are tragic. Countless students are knowingly assigned to schools with unswerving track records of failure and nearly certain prospects of continued failure.

In the 2007–8 school year, California, Georgia, and Maryland had a total of 392 schools that were beyond the critical "year five" of NCLB improvement status, when fundamental restructuring was supposed to solve the problem. Forty of these schools were in year eight of failure or beyond. The Maryland State Department of Education tried to wrestle away eleven of these schools from the control of the Baltimore City Public School system; each of the schools had at least nine consecutive years of poor performance. [19]

The success rate of NCLB's interventions should come as no surprise. Previous research has revealed similarly discouraging findings on a whole host of improvement efforts. A 2003 analysis of the Schools Under Registration Review (SURR) process in New York found that half of schools didn't improve at all, and for those that did, the improvements "do not assure that anywhere near enough of their students possess sufficient academic skills to pass, much less excel on, state tests."[20]

A study of state takeovers of failing schools and districts noted that they "have yet to produce dramatic consistent increases in student performance." It found that though takeovers might cause commotion among adults, the impact on student learning typically "falls short of expectations." Takeovers "seem to be yielding more gains in central office activities than in classroom instructional practices."[21] Similar results were found in state-driven reconstitution efforts, the success rate of which is "limited."[22]

A review of more than one hundred books, articles, briefs, and more on turnaround efforts concluded, "There is, at present, no strong evidence that any particular intervention type works most of the time or in most places."[23] Looking back on the lengthy list of attempted interventions, one set of experts concluded: "Turnaround efforts have for the most part resulted in only marginal improvements . . . Promising practices have failed to work at scale when imported to troubled schools."[24]

Perhaps the best summary of this mountain of findings was provided by Tom Loveless in his Brookings study of persistent failure in California's lowest performing schools. "Achievement seems to be part of the institutional DNA of schools, handed down from decade to decade, the past influencing the future."

FLAILING IN THE DARK

Despite years of effort and great expenditures of time, money, and energy, we still lack basic information about which tactics will make a struggling school excellent. As a 2003 report on fixing failing schools noted, "Surprisingly little is known about what kinds of interventions are most likely to turn faltering schools into successful education institutions."[25]

A study that sought to compare California's low-performing schools that failed to make progress to its low-performing schools that did improve came to a confounding conclusion: Clear differences avoided detection. Writing about the schools that failed to improve, the authors noted, "These were schools in the same cities and districts, often serving children from the same backgrounds. Some of them also adopted the same curriculum programs, had teachers with similar backgrounds, and had similar opportunities for professional development."[26]

Several years later, "A Call to Restructure Restructuring" reached a parallel conclusion. "None of the staff we interviewed in schools that had exited restructuring could point to a single strategy that they believed was the key to improving student achievement."

In Ohio, numerous strategies were employed to improve failing schools, including new reading and math programs, academic coaches, and staff changes. With little to show for the efforts, an urban district's spokesman conceded, "If there were a simple model you could just plop down and say, 'This is what you'd do,' everybody would have done it already."[27]

Nancy Grasmick served as Maryland's state superintendent for twenty years. In addition to working closely with two large struggling urban districts, she was a leader in the accountability movement. She has written: "Given Maryland's fifteen-year history of school reform and accountability, the state has plenty of experience with comprehensive reform models."

Nevertheless, she acknowledges that turnaround solutions remain elusive. "Very little research exists on how to bring about real sea change in schools...Clearly, there's no infallible strategy or even sequence of them."[28] In response to the growing number of failing schools in Baltimore, she said, "No one has the answer. It's like finding the cure for cancer."[29]

Even the nation's extensive experience with NCLB restructuring has failed to uncover answers. Despite thousands of interventions, each restructuring option has failed to generate promising results, and none has emerged as the best of the bunch. The Center on Education Policy analysis concluded, "There is no statistical reason to suspect that any one of the federal restructuring options is more effective than another in helping schools make AYP."

A 2003 study reached the same conclusion: "No particular intervention appears more successful than any other."[30] A number of studies, rather than admitting that no answer exists, spin these findings, reporting, "context matters" and "one size does not fit all."[31] Other researchers have openly lamented the lack of reliable information explaining successful efforts.[32] The literature has been described as "sparse" and "scarce"; one study noted the "dearth of evidence."[33]

Consequently, those attempting to help others fix broken schools have typically resorted to identifying activities in improved schools, such as improving data collection and communicating a positive vision.[34] However, this case-study style of analysis is deeply flawed. As the U.S. Department of Education's study noted, reports "that look back at factors that may have contributed to (a) school's success" are "particularly weak in determining causal validity for several reasons, including the fact that there is no way to be confident that the features common to successful turnaround schools are not also common to schools that fail."

This lack of information explains the clashing policies emanating from states. Some encouraged schools to use turnaround specialists, while at least one state banned that as an intervention. Some states encouraged schools to make use of the "other" option under NCLB restructuring, while other states discouraged its use in favor of state-defined interventions.[35]

The federal government itself has acknowledged the field's ignorance. As the Center on Education Policy reported, "The NCLB law does not specify any additional actions for schools that remain in the implementation phase of restructuring for more than one year (past year five), and (the department) has offered little guidance on what to do about persistently struggling schools." Even in its "Turning Around Chronically Low-Performing Schools" practice guide, purportedly a resource for states and districts, the department conceded, "All recommendations had to rely on low levels of evidence" because it could not identify any rigorous studies finding that "specific turnaround practices produce significantly better academic outcomes."

We not only lack a strategy for persistently failing schools, we don't even have a roadmap.

STILL IN ITS INFANCY?

Some have argued that the abject failure of turnarounds to date simply means we need to keep looking for solutions. The problem, many suggest, is that we haven't put sufficient time, effort, or thought into finding the answer. Some have observed, "Turnaround at scale is still in its infancy," and, "In education, turnarounds have been tried rarely."[36] Others report optimistically, "Over time, as experience and research accumulates, it will be possible to zero in on stories of school turnarounds that were sustained over time."[37]

But the number and scope of fix-it efforts have been extraordinary. As Hess and others have noted, this work has been underway for four decades, with numerous "movements" coming and going, such as new curricula, "effective schools" models, and accountability. Even before NCLB, significant interventions were already underway. In 2002, twenty-four states had authority to take over districts with failing schools. In 1989, New Jersey took over Jersey City Public Schools, in 1995 it took over Newark Public Schools. In 1993, California took over the Compton Unified School District. In 1995, Ohio took over Cleveland Public Schools.

In 2002, fifteen states had the power to take over individual schools. In 2000, Alabama took over a number of schools, and Maryland seized control of three schools in Baltimore. Nineteen states were authorized to require the reconstitution of failing schools. Between 1993 and 1997, such interventions took place in Denver, Chicago, New York City, and Houston.[38]

Since NCLB, interventions have only grown in number and intensity. In 2006–7, schools in "corrective action" (year three of improvement status) implemented numerous remedies. More than 750 schools implemented a new research-based curriculum, more than seven hundred used an outside expert to advise the school, nearly four hundred restructured the internal organization of the school, and more than two hundred extended the school day or school year. More than three hundred either replaced staff members and/or the principal—among the toughest interventions possible.[39]

Many have noted that once schools reach NCLB restructuring, rather than using one of the law's stated interventions, they choose the "other" option, under which they have flexibility to design an improvement strategy of their choosing. Critics charge that districts use this "loophole" to avoid tough tactics in favor of cosmetic changes. This, critics argue, explains the ineffectiveness of the restructuring.

As scholar Chester E. Finn, Jr., said, "Because the most intrusive and disruptive makeovers are politically and bureaucratically unpalatable, every state and district has nearly always picked the least intrusive option. You shouldn't be surprised that the schools aren't much better; the interventions aren't very strong."[40]

It is true that the "other" option has been the most commonly used intervention. The Center on Education Policy found that among the five states investigated, selection of the "other" option ranged from 86 percent to 96 percent. But even these states tried a number of NCLB's listed "tougher" interventions in some cases. Both Maryland and California replaced all or some of the staff at more than 10 percent of their failing schools. They and other states also turned over the operation of some schools to outside organizations. These tactics, however, proved just as ineffective as the presumably "softer" interventions used under the "other" option.[41]

Even under the maligned "other" option, districts have tried an astonishing array of strategies. These include different types of school-level needs assessments, surveys of school staff, conferences, professional development, turnaround specialists, school improvement committees, training sessions, principal mentors, teacher coaches, leadership facilitators, instructional trainers, subject matter experts, audits, summer residential academies, student tutoring, research-based reform models, reconfigured grade spans, alternative governance models, new curricula, improved use of data, and much more.

It's simply impossible to argue that turnaround efforts haven't been given a chance.

KEEP DIGGING

Despite this overwhelming evidence, rather than jettisoning the turnaround mindset, many advocate for new improvement efforts. Grasmick supported recognizing turnarounds as a discipline within education.[42] Hess and Gift have argued for developing "a set of effective operators capable of contracting with multiple districts or states to provide the oversight, leadership, knowledge, and personnel to drive restructuring."[43] Hassel and Hassel have recommended that states and districts "fuel the pipeline" of K–12 turnaround leaders.[44]

The Education Commission of the States has embraced the idea of cultivating turnaround leaders, and NewSchools Venture Fund has advocated for the creation of "turnaround management organizations."[45] The research firm Mass Insight recommends creating a "new framework" for turnarounds, one that empowers the right people, clusters needy schools, and builds external leadership structures to facilitate change.[46] The Center on Education Policy has recommended NCLB be amended to allow additional turnaround strategies.

The federal government has also bought into the turnaround craze. Secretary of Education Arne Duncan made turnarounds a central part of the Race to the Top and repeatedly asked Congress for increased appropriations for turnarounds. In the 2009 federal stimulus legislation, $3.5 billion were appropriated for federal School Improvement Grants. The administration requested an additional $1.5 billion for this program in the 2010 budget. These dollars are in addition to the numerous streams of existing federal funds that can be used to address failing schools.

The dissonance is deafening. Experience tells us emphatically that we can't rely on turnaround efforts. Why the stubborn insistence on continuing to do so?

MISUNDERSTANDING THE LESSONS OF HIGH-PERFORMING, HIGH-POVERTY SCHOOLS

The most common—but also the most deeply flawed—justification for continuing turnarounds is that there are high-performing schools in American cities. That is, proponents point to successful urban schools and then infer that scalable turnaround strategies are possible. It has become fashionable to repeat philosopher Emmanuel Kant's adage that "the actual proves the possible."

A newspaper article scolding Boston for not improving its failing schools pointed out the "clear evidence...that it is possible to build great public schools in poor areas."[47] The research organization Mass Insight began its study of turnarounds by looking for "proof points—evidence that public schools could bring highly challenged, high poverty students to achievement levels matching those of their high-performing suburban counterparts." They ultimately became convinced of the viability of turnarounds in part because of the "promise of high-performing high-poverty school success." The National Association of State Boards of Education built its playbook for transforming low-performing schools on the example of already high-performing schools.[48]

As was shown in chapter 3 and will be shown again in chapters 6 and 9, it is undoubtedly the case that there are high-performing, high-poverty urban schools. But having excellent schools is not the same as fixing failing schools. These are wholly different enterprises. As one study explained, "Much is known about how effective schools work, but it is far less clear how to move an ineffective school from failure to success...*Being* a high-performing school and *becoming* a high-performing school are very different challenges."[49]

As more people are realizing, America's superior urban schools "are virtually always new starts rather than schools that were previously underperforming."[50] Education philanthropist Bill Gates has noted that the highest-performing, high-poverty schools were started anew via chartering, they weren't fixed failing schools. "We had less success trying to change an existing school than helping to create a new school."[51] Indeed, the newspaper article on Boston referenced earlier discussed two examples of very high-performing schools that were proving disadvantaged urban students could excel. Both were newly started charters, not turnarounds.

Probably the most convincing argument for the difference between start-ups and turnarounds comes from those actually running high-performing, high-poverty urban schools. The most successful school operators like KIPP and Achievement First open *new* schools; they don't reform failing schools. KIPP's lone foray into turnarounds, Cole College Prep in Denver, was a failure. In response, KIPP's spokesman said, "Our core competency is starting and running new schools."[52]

A 2006 NewSchools Venture Fund study confirmed the widespread aversion to takeover-and-turnaround strategies among successful school operators; it found "only tepid interest" among these leaders. Only four of thirty-six organizations interviewed expressed interest in school restructuring.[53] Similarly, when San Diego sought high-performing operators to take over several failing schools in 2004, it launched a recruitment operation with the California Charter Schools Association. Only one entity showed interest.[54]

In the NewSchools study, nearly every potential operator said that starting fresh was preferable. One compared turnarounds to "putting old wine in new bottles." "It is much better to work with new schools from the get-go rather than have to turn everything around after it is failing already."

The three findings from above deserve repeating: First, fix-it efforts have consistently failed. Second, our knowledge base about improving failing schools is staggeringly small. Third, exceptional urban schools are virtually always start-ups or consistently excellent schools—not drastically improved, once-failing schools.

So when considering turnarounds we should stop repeating "the actual proves the possible" and bear in mind a different Kant adage: "Ought implies can." If we are going to tell states and districts that they must fix all of their failing schools, or if we are to consider it a moral obligation to radically improve such schools, we should be certain that this endeavor is possible. But there is no reason to believe that it is.

This conclusion isn't defeatist, nor is it an indictment of public education or those working in it. The inability to fundamentally alter and improve persistent failures isn't unique to public education: "Research on and experience with public-school turnarounds closely echo much of the research on turnarounds in the business, nonprofit, and other public sectors."[55]

LOOKING BEYOND EDUCATION

Other industries also produce chronic low-performers. They also have tried to devise fix-it strategies. But the majority of these turnaround efforts fail. Unfortunately, education leaders seem to believe that "turnaround" is a fertile field. But those familiar with the true private-sector track record have advised otherwise: "There is a risk that politicians, government officials, and others, newly enamored of the language of failure and turnaround and inadequately informed of the empirical evidence and practical experience in the for-profit sector...will have unrealistic expectations of the transformative power of the turnaround process."[56]

As in education, the lack of success hasn't been for a lack of trying. As Mass Insight reported, "For all of that research on effective practices in cross-sector turnaround, and for all of that turnaround management organizational capacity, the record for successful corporate and nonprofit turnaround is not great." One business scholar concurred: "Failure to sustain significant change recurs again and again despite substantial resources committed to the change effort (many are bankrolled by top management), talented and committed people 'driving the change,' and high stakes."[57]

Hess and Gift reviewed the success rates of Total Quality Management (TQM) and Business Process Reengineering (BPR), two common approaches to organizational reform in the private sector. The literature suggests that both have failed to generate the results desired two-thirds of the time or more.[58] BPR appears to have success rates as low as 25 percent.[59] Elsewhere it has been estimated that "even the most intensive turnaround interventions" succeed only slightly more often.[60]

As Hess and Gift concluded, "The hope that we can systematically turn around all troubled schools—or even a majority of them—is at odds with much of what we know from similar efforts in the private sector." We may actually need to even consider the discouraging turnaround success rates from the business world beyond the reach of urban districts. Many have noted that flexibility and dynamism are hardwired into private businesses. Free markets provide them great flexibility, and, as a result, they continuously react to the decisions of other enterprises, navigate shifting consumer demands, and more.

So we should expect this environment to be more hospitable than what Hess refers to as the "political, regulatory, and contractual morass of K–12 schooling." As one study put it, "If private firms, which are built to respond to competition, are unable to make this kind of leap, we can't expect gigantic, byzantine school systems, which are insulated from competition, shackled by union contracts, and constrained by a sticky web of regulations, to do so."[61]

Another complication arises from public education's differences from the private sector. Whereas private employees have an enormous incentive to keep their firms from failing due to the threat of job loss, employees in the public sector are typically insulated from such fears. Consequently, "performance decline poses only a limited or nominal threat to organizational existence or to individuals careers...this means that the cost of failure may often be quite low for some stakeholders."[62]

In total, then, looking outside of education should only heighten our misgivings about turnarounds. A consultant with the Bridgespan Group said, "Turnarounds in the public education space are far harder than any turnaround I've ever seen in the for-profit space."[63] Similarly, a 2005 study concluded, "While turnarounds are difficult in the private sector, they may be even more challenging in schools."[64]

Understanding the unreliability of turnarounds is critical to advancing portfolio management. Efforts to fix cannot be the primary strategy for addressing entities chronically on the far left of the quality distribution. Other industries have internalized this lesson by developing other tactics for dealing with persistent failures, namely finding a way to bring them to an end. The equivalent for education is closing long-failing schools.

Many have raised concerns with this analogy, arguing that such an approach is incompatible with public schooling. Noting that businesses often close and that their customers can easily go elsewhere, one analysis concluded, "The schools world is different in this respect. The students still need to be served."[65] Similarly, the Center on Education Policy concluded, "States and districts cannot simply close all these struggling schools and still maintain their obligation to provide public education to all children."

But this analysis ignores that closures are only one part of an integrated system of portfolio management. Closures are a single element of an ongoing process that includes new starts and expansions of high-performing entities. The industry survives and thrives not by remaining static, but by replacing failed entities with new and better ones.

The question for urban public education is whether it can create a coordinated system that compensates for the loss of failing schools by continuously generating new and better schools. If such a system is possible, can it be executed in a way that preserves the most important features of public education, such as public oversight and the guarantee that every student will have access to high-quality schools?

Yes.

The following section introduces chartering, the mechanism by which such a system can be brought about. The final section of the book describes the process of implementing chartering's four key innovations to build the urban school system of the future.

NOTES

1. Ted Kolderie, *Creating the Capacity for Change: How and Why Legislatures Are Opening a New-Schools Sector in Public Education* (Bethesda, MD: Education Week Press, 2004), 62.

2. See Joe Graba, "We Cannot Get the Schools We Need by Changing the Schools We Have" (paper presented at Grantmakers in Education/Philanthropy Roundtable meeting, Denver, Colorado, May 26–27, 2004), http://www.educationevolving.org/pdf/Graba_Presentation.pdf.

3. See Clayton Christensen, *The Innovator's Dilemma: When New Technologies Cause Great Firms to Fail* (Boston: Harvard Business School Press, 1997), and Clayton Christensen, Michael B. Hern, and Curtis W. Johnson, *Disrupting Class: How Disruptive Innovation Will Change the Way the World Learns* (New York: McGraw Hill, 2008).

4. Andrew Calkins, "School Turnaround: What It Is and Why We Need It" (paper presented at American Enterprise Institute/Mass Insight Education & Research Institute Conference, "Turning Around the Nation's Worst Schools," Washington, DC, March 11, 2008), 1.

5. *California's Lowest-Performing Schools: Who They Are, the Challenges They Face, and How They're Improving* (Palo Alto, CA: EdSource, 2003), 1.

6. Jennifer Smith Richards, "Reborn Schools Disappoint: Big Changes Have Brought Only Modest Results," *Columbus Dispatch*, January 25, 2009.

7. Tom Loveless, *The 2009 Brown Center Report on American Education: How Well Are American Students Learning?* (Washington, DC: The Brookings Institution, March 2010).

8. David. A Stuit, *Are Bad Schools Immortal?* (Washington, DC: Thomas B. Fordham Institute, December 2010).

9. See Andrew Calkins, et al., *The Turnaround Challenge: Why America's Best Opportunity to Dramatically Improve Student Achievement Lies in Our Worst-Performing Schools* (Boston: Mass Insight Education and Research Institute, 2007), http://arkansased.org/pdf/sarg_g_challenge_092107.pdf ; and Kieran Walshe, et al., "Organizational Failure and Turnaround: Lessons for Public Services from the For-Profit Sector," *Public Money & Management* 24, no. 4 (August 2004): 201.

10. See Naresh Pandit, "Some Recommendations for Improved Research on Corporate Turnaround," *Management* 3, no. 2 (2000): 31–56.

11. Seth Reynolds, "Turnaround Strategies and Attempts So Far" (paper presented American Enterprise Institute/Mass Insight Education & Research Institute Conference, "Turning around the Nation's Worst Schools," Washington, DC, March 11, 2008), 36.

12. Dana Brinson, Julie Kowal, and Bryan Hassel, *School Turnarounds: Actions and Results*, Center on Innovation & Improvement (Chapel Hill, NC: Public Impact, 2008), 5.

13. Calkins, et al., *The Turnaround Challenge*, 4.

14. University of Virginia, Darden School of Business, School Turnaround Specialist Program, http://darden.virginia.edu/web/Darden-Curry-PLE/UVA-School-Turnaround/Program/ , last updated December 31, 2011.

15. *State and Local Implementation of the No Child Left Behind Act: Volume III—Accountability Under NCLB: Interim Report* (Washington, DC: Office of Planning, Evaluation and Development, Policy and Program Studies Service, U.S. Department of Education, 2007).

16. See California state report in Xiang, Cronin, and Dahlin, *The Accountability Illusion*, 1.

17. Sara Mead, "Easy Way Out: 'Restructured' Usually Means Little Has Changed" *EducationNext* 7, no. 1 (Winter 2007), 59.

18. Xiang, Cronin, and Dahlin, *The Accountability Illusion.*

19. Liz Bowie and Sara Neufeld, "Md Acts to Seize 11 City Schools: Grasmick Seeks Control under No Child Left Behind," *Baltimore Sun*, March 29, 2006.

20. Ronald C. Brady, "Can Failing Schools Be Fixed?" (Washington, DC: Thomas B. Fordham Institute, January 2003), 23.

21. Todd Ziebarth, "State Takeovers and Reconstitutions," ECS Policy Brief (Denver, CO: Education Commission of the States, April 2002), 2–3.

22. Ziebarth, "State Takeovers and Reconstitutions;" Brady, "Can Failing Schools Be Fixed?"

23. Brady, "Can Failing Schools Be Fixed?"

24. Frederick M. Hess, et al., "Introductory Letter" (paper presented at American Enterprise Institute/Mass Insight Education & Research Institute Conference, "Turning around the Nation's Worst Schools," Washington, D.C., March 11, 2008).

25. Brady, "Can Failing Schools Be Fixed?"

26. *California's Lowest-Performing Schools*, 1.

27. Richards, "Reborn Schools Disappoint."

28. Nancy Grasmick, "NCLB's Impact on Turnarounds: A Policymaker's Perspective" (paper presented at American Enterprise Institute/Mass Insight Education & Research Institute Conference, "Turning Around the Nation's Worst Schools," Washington, DC, March 11, 2008).

29. Quoted in David J. Hoff, "Schools Struggling to Meet Key Goal on Accountability: Number Failing to Make AYP Rises to 28 Percent," *Education Week*, January 7, 2009.

30. Brady, "Can Failing Schools Be Fixed?"

31. Christopher Corallo and Deborah H. McDonald, *What Works with Low-Performing Schools: A Review of Research* (Charleston, WV: AEL, January 2002), 17.

32. See Julia M. Kowal and Emily Ayscue Hassel, *Turnarounds with New Leaders and Staff*, The Center for Comprehensive School Reform and Improvement (Washington, DC: Learning Point Associates, 2005).

33. Ziebarth, "State Takeovers and Reconstitutions;" Brinson, Kowal, and Hassel, *School Turnarounds: Actions and Results*; Herman, et al., *Turning Around Chronically Low-Performing Schools*.

34. See Brinson, Kowal, and Hassel, *School Turnarounds: Actions and Results*; Emily Ayscue Hassel and Bryan Hassel, "The Big U-Turn: How to Bring Schools from the Brink of Doom to Stellar Success," *EducationNext* 9, no. 1, Winter 2009; *From Sanctions to Solutions: Meeting the Needs of Low-Performing Schools—The Report of the NASBE Study Group on Low-Performing Schools from Sanctions to Solutions* (Alexandria, VA: National Association of State Boards of Education, 2002).

35. Scott, "A Call to Restructure Restructuring."

36. Reynolds, "Turnaround Strategies and Attempts So Far;" Hassel and Hassel, "The Big U-Turn."

37. Brinson, Kowal, and Hassel, *School Turnarounds: Actions and Results*.

38. Ziebarth, "State Takeovers and Reconstitutions."

39. Data available in Consolidated State Performance Reports, U.S. Department of Education, http://www2.ed.gov/admins/lead/account/consolidated/index.html.

40. Quoted in Michael Jonas, "Held Back," *CommonWealth*, November 2008, 37.

41. Scott, "A Call to Restructure Restructuring."

42. Grasmick, "NCLB's Impact on Turnarounds." This view is shared by research organization Mass Insight; see Calkins, et al., *The Turnaround Challenge*.

43. Frederick M. Hess and Thomas Gift, "School Turnarounds: Resisting the Hype, Giving Them Hope," *Education Outlook* #2 (Washington, DC: American Enterprise Institute for Public Policy Research, February 2009), 4.

44. Hassel and Hassel, "The Big U-Turn."

45. Todd Ziebarth and Bryan Hassel, "School Restructuring via the No Child Left Behind Act: Potential State Roles," ECS Policy Brief (Denver, CO: Education Commission of the States, November 2005); "Considering School Turnarounds: Market Research and Analysis" (Boston, MA: Mass Insight Education and Research Institute, March 2007), 37.

46. Calkins et al., *The Turnaround Challenge*, 4. See also William Guenther, "Effective Turnaround at Scale: A Framework" (paper presented at American Enterprise Institute/Mass Insight Education & Research Institute Conference, "Turning around the Nation's Worst Schools," Washington, DC, March 11, 2008), 22.

47. Michael Jonas, "The Answer: Fifteen Years into Education Reform, We Are Still Failing to Fix the Most Troubled Schools. Now There's No Excuse," *The Boston Globe*, June 1, 2008.

48. *From Sanctions to Solution*.

49. Brady, "Can Failing Schools Be Fixed?"

50. Remarkably, this statement came from a paper arguing for another new turnaround strategy. Though appreciating that start-ups, not turnarounds, are the pathway to success, the researcher recommends more turnarounds.

51. Bill Gates, "2009 Annual Letter from Bill Gates: U.S. Education," Bill and Melinda Gates Foundation, http://www.gatesfoundation.org/annual-letter/Pages/2009-united-states-education.aspx.

52. David Whitman, *Sweating the Small Stuff: Inner-City Schools and the New Paternalism*, (Washington, DC: The Thomas B. Fordham Institute, June 2008), 189–90.

53. "Considering School Turnarounds," 29–30.

54. Joe Williams and Thomas Toch, "Extreme Makeover: Two Failing San Diego Schools Get New Start as Charters," *Ideas at Work* (Washington, DC: Education Sector, November 2006), 2.

55. Kowal and Hassel, *Turnarounds with New Leaders and Staff.*

56. Walshe, et al., "Organizational Failure and Turnaround."

57. Peter Senge, et al., *The Dance of Change: The Challenges of Sustaining Momentum in Learning Organizations* (New York: Doubleday, 1999), 6.

58. Hess and Gift, "School Turnarounds: Resisting the Hype."

59. Frederick M. Hess and Thomas Gift, "How to Turn Schools Around," *American School Board Journal*, November 2008.

60. Hess, et al., "Introductory Letter."

61. Andy Smarick, "Wave of the Future: Why Charter Schools Should Replace Failing Urban Schools," *EducationNext* 8, no. 1 (Winter 2008), 43.

62. Walshe, et al., "Organizational Failure and Turnaround."

63. Quoted in Rosemary Kendrick, "Turning Around America's Worst Schools," *The American*, April 8, 2008, http://www.american.com/archive/2008/april-04-08/turning-around-america2019s-worst-schools.

64. Kowal and Hassel, *Turnarounds with New Leaders and Staff.*

65. Calkins, "School Turnaround: What It Is and Why We Need It."

Part II

Urban Charter Schooling

In the fall of 1992, on the east side of St. Paul, Minnesota, City Academy High School opened its doors to students for the first time. In many ways it was like other public schools in the Twin Cities and for that matter across the nation. It was a public school through and through, funded by the government, tuition-free, and non-discriminatory. It had no entrance exam. It was part of the state's public school system in all senses and accountable for its results.

Little did its teachers and students know they were helping launch the most important systemic reform in U.S. K–12 education since the development of common schools nearly 150 years earlier. Though chartering was conceived as a way to develop new, highly accountable public schools and eventually became the primary means of providing public educational alternatives, its potential is even greater.

Chartering offers a competing and superior vision for the delivery of public education in urban America. It differs from the long dominant and unsuccessful district system in important ways, demonstrating that many current arrangements assumed to be essential are anything but. Most importantly, its key features will enable us to properly manage city school portfolios in a way that will create dynamic, responsive, high-performing, self-improving systems of urban education.

Chapter 5

The Charter Revolution

To appreciate the revolution of chartering, you must first understand the district.

Despite America's enormous diversity and tradition of local control of schools, for a century, the district has been the nation's single system for delivering public education.

In the years after the mid-nineteenth century development of "common" schools, cities wrestled with the best way to administer public education. Governance and management systems varied significantly. Generally, a central organization had some power over spending and a number of administrative details.[1] But through the late 1800s, a city's local conditions and individual personalities determined a great deal.[2] As education historian Diane Ravitch has written, "At century's end, there was no American educational 'system.'"[3]

But around the turn of the twentieth century, cities began adopting a common model for overseeing their public schools. Education historian David B. Tyack would later name this arrangement—with irony—"the one best system." In nearly all locations, it was the product of progressive community leaders who wanted non-partisan, good government run by "professionals." They sought to remove politics from schools. They opposed political-machine influence on public education, and many harbored misgivings about the effects of mass immigration.

They also bemoaned the lack of sophistication and organization of public school systems. In Ravitch's words, "In an age marked by the development of systems and organization, the schools seemed helter-skelter, lacking uniformity or standards."[4] To reformers, the solution was to put "experts" in charge and require that systems adopt the tidy, sensible management features of large corporations. Reformers were impressed by the order and efficiency of "the division of labor in the factory, the punctuality of the railroad, the chain of command and coordination in modern businesses."[5]

Centralizing decision-making in a bureaucracy run by education professionals would help bring "scientific management" to schools, thereby improving performance and increasing efficiency.[6] Despite the opposition of those who saw such proposals as elitist and anti-immigrant, progressive reformers triumphed in city after city. Upon gaining power, they typically removed authority from wards and neighborhoods and consolidated power in a large central entity, installing the community's "best men" as school board members and superintendents.

Urban school systems grew in size and complexity and became vastly more hierarchical, their schools more uniform. The previous era of decentralization and variety, that arguably suited America's pluralistic democracy, gave way to an efficient, "rational," top-down, and highly standardized school system.

Urban public schools were organized into geographically large districts. This was accomplished through consolidation and centralization. Nationwide, the number of districts decreased rapidly though enrollment skyrocketed.[7] Districts were governed by school boards, whose members were typically elected. The boards were smaller and more "professional" than those of the previous era. They functioned like K–12 versions of corporate boards; they developed policies, approved textbooks, maintained buildings, and hired the executives.

The district superintendent, like a public school's CEO, led the system's bureaucracy, hiring staff, overseeing schools, and implementing board directives. As these systems grew and became more complex, the central office expanded; the number of central office "supervisors" and administrators soared.[8]

An important feature of this central apparatus was its complete control over its schools. It hired principals and employed teachers. It negotiated contracts, determined calendars, and more. This can be thought of as the district's "vertical consolidation." It controlled every meaningful element of its schools.

The most important characteristic, however, was the district's role as the sole provider of public education in its designated area; scholar Ted Kolderie aptly refers to districts as "territorial exclusive franchises."[9] If there were a public K–12 school within its borders, it belonged to the school district. This can be thought of as its "horizontal consolidation."

None of the significant changes to public education in the twentieth century fundamentally altered the district's dominance. Not *Brown vs. Board of Education*, not Sputnik, not unionization. The growing list of federal education programs actually helped entrench this system by treating districts as the primary policy driver and recipient of federal funds.

In rare instances, parts of this formula were adjusted. A failing district may have been taken over by the state, a principal may have been given greater control over her staff, or community groups may have gained more say in a school's decision making. But these were exceptions to the rule, and they were typically fleeting.

The district system was so ubiquitous for so long that, to most observers, it became synonymous with public education. As Tyack noted more than three decades ago, though it was borne of heated battles over power and values, this system became so familiar as to seem inevitable. Rather than defining public schooling as a set of principles (tuition-free, non-discriminatory, etc.), that could be actualized in myriad ways, it came to be seen as a structure—a board- and superintendent-led entity completely operating all of an area's public schools.

But with massive evidence that urban districts have continuously failed to provide city kids with an adequate education, it's fair to wonder whether this unitary structure might have something to do with such comprehensive failure. But even if the answer is yes, is there any legitimate alternative? Is it possible to maintain the principles of public education while altering the structure through which it has been traditionally delivered?

Or, as scholar Joe Graba put it, can we keep the faith while reforming the church?

A NEW TYPE OF SCHOOL

In the 1970s and 1980s, an idea began to emerge about running some public schools differently. Several thinkers seem to have developed similar ideas independently, and then after some cross-pollination, views coalesced around a hybrid.

Ray Budde, a career educator, is often credited with hatching one of the key concepts. He suggested that schools, rather than being run remotely from a district office, be managed by those in classrooms. A group of teachers would be given a "charter" by the school board; they would take control of an existing school and be responsible for its operations. [10]

Similar ideas were percolating in Chicago. Joe Loftus, from the Center for Child Welfare Strategy, proposed that the school system's lowest-performing three percent of schools be turned into "charter schools" annually.

They would be run by private entities and monitored for quality by an independent board.[11] At about the same time, a group of California educators argued that teachers should be empowered to start their own public schools.[12]

Though these ideas didn't immediately catch fire, they were eventually noticed by an important player. Albert Shanker, president of the American Federation of Teachers (AFT), wanted to give teachers more say in how schools were run. He believed, "American education could not be reformed until teachers could determine the form and concept of schooling."

In a 1988 National Press Club speech, Shanker floated an idea similar to Budde's: That teachers be empowered to operate their own schools. With the permission of a school's staff, a group of teachers would create an autonomous program within the school's walls. It would be a choice-based program—parents would have the option of enrolling their children in the new school-within-a-school.[13]

Three months later, Shanker explained his ideas more fully in a column in the *New York Times*. Reporting that AFT delegates had embraced the concept at their annual convention, Shanker encouraged boards and unions to begin developing a process by which teachers could have their proposals for new schools considered and authorized. Citing Budde, he recommended the name "charter schools."

Proposed school characteristics were pulled directly from Budde's published work. An official government body would authorize schools, teams of teachers would receive the charter, the schools would develop innovative programs, parents would have choice, the schools would have equal funding and budgetary discretion, and the schools' results would be fully transparent.[14] Shanker's lone substantive variation, subtle but ultimately portentous, was that the schools be newly created, not reformed existing schools.

Unlike many other promising proposals, charter schools were fortunate to slip through a "policy window," find fertile ground, and grow roots. A series of fortuitous circumstances pushed Minnesota to the forefront of chartering. In the 1970s, the state allowed several alternative schools to open and later experimented with inter-district open enrollment and post-secondary options for high school students.[15] As a result, Minnesotans saw that school choice had important benefits and that the apocalyptic claims of choice opponents were unfounded.[16]

For years, Minnesota's Citizens League had played an important role in education innovation, including issuing a positive report on choice and recommending the creation of schools that would give teachers increased decision-making authority.[17] The League convened a committee in 1987 to consider the state's urban schools and, after becoming aware of Budde's and Shanker's ideas, included these in the committee's work. Shanker's presentation to the group on the charter concept in October 1988 heightened interest among participants.

In November, the Citizens League published its final report, "Chartered Schools = Choices for Educators + Quality for All Students." It recommended that Minnesota allow districts and the state to create charter schools, which would be public schools run by licensed teachers. The schools would be free to "pursue different education routes" but would be required to meet accreditation standards.

The freedom of schools to develop unique programs was particularly important to the committee. Striking a blow at the district system, the report argued, "Teachers and schools should adapt to children's needs rather than requiring children to adapt to the standard system." The report was recommending the creation of new schools that would operate outside of the district while adhering to the principles of public education. [18]

The report made its way to a few state representatives, and the core concept survived several years of legislative wrangling. A provision allowing for this new type of school was included in 1991 legislation, which Governor Arne Carlson signed into law. In many ways, the statute resembles modern-day charter legislation: A nonsectarian, tuition-free school is authorized by an approved sponsor; the school is free of many traditional regulations; a contract describes the school's program and performance measures; the sponsor can close the schools for underperformance.

But compared to today's laws, the original had a number of curious characteristics. The word "charter" never appears; instead, they are referred to as "outcome-based schools." Only licensed teachers were allowed to start them, and a majority of each school's board of directors had to be teachers employed by the school. The law allowed only eight schools to be opened.

The first to take advantage of the law was City Academy High School, opening in fall 1992, sponsored by St. Paul District #625 and the Minnesota Department of Education. But soon the law's influence extended far beyond the state's borders. Over time, as charters expanded across the country and state and federal policies evolved, chartering showed it had the potential to become an extraordinarily powerful force in public education.

THE EVOLUTION OF CHARTERING

A year after the passage of Minnesota's law, California adopted a very similar statute. Then the floodgates opened. In 1993, six states passed laws. Over the next few years, a steady stream of states would join them; by 1998, thirty-five states had charter laws. Soon enabling legislation evolved. States passing laws for the first time looked to the experiences of veteran states, and states with experience amended their laws to reflect lessons learned. Changes included improving funding, extending the length of charter contracts, and helping schools acquire facilities.[19]

The most important shifts were in the entities empowered to authorize charter schools and the number of schools allowed in each state. Many states' first charter laws limited authorizing to district school boards. This reflected, first, state legislatures' loyalty to the ingrained practice of having all public schools emanate from districts and, second, districts' aversion to relinquishing their "territorial exclusive franchise."

However, districts were often unwilling authorizers, viewing charters as competition; accordingly, they typically permitted few if any charters to open. Often districts were unskilled authorizers, having been designed to control all aspects of schools, not monitor them from arm's length. Consequently, states began expanding the pool of eligible authorizers. Minnesota and Ohio included institutions of higher education and nonprofits. Florida, Colorado, and the District of Columbia created state-level authorizers. Indiana gave the mayor of Indianapolis authorizing authority. Many states lifted caps on the number of charter schools allowed.

When Minnesota's charters proved popular, the legislature raised the cap beyond the original eight schools. Texas expanded the number allowed soon after its first law passed.[20] When chartering proved successful in New York City, the state doubled the number of charters allowed. When late-arriving Maryland passed its first law in 2003, no cap was included. These two changes were by no means comprehensive; some states maintained caps and/ or limited authorizing to local boards. But these trends began to show that chartering was more than just a tool to start a few new schools.

As state policies evolved, the federal government slowly took interest in chartering, eventually settling on two areas of activity. Though state and local funding formulas could be adjusted to provide charters comparable operating support, there weren't programs to address the costs associated with starting a new school. In advance of opening, charters needed money to recruit teachers, design programs, and more.

In 1991, David Durenberger, a Republican U.S. senator from Minnesota, introduced what eventually became known as the "charter school grant program," federal aid for "start-up" grants. The program was adopted in 1994. The second area was facilities. State and local rules seldom provided charters with buildings; so affording facilities became the sector's tallest obstacle. The federal government created two programs to address this challenge, one that encouraged states to provide facilities aid, the other to support innovative loan programs. By the end of 2009, the federal government had invested $2.5 billion through these three programs.

These state and federal activities had a profound influence. The National Alliance for Public Charter Schools reported that in the fall of 2011, there were 5,600 charters serving 2 million students nationwide. But the aggregate figures mask the most noteworthy feature of chartering's expansion: the concentration of charters in urban America. In the last twenty years, nothing has had a more profound influence on the options available to city students.

CHARTERING AND AMERICA'S CITIES

Because chartering is simply a process by which new schools can be created and monitored, it provides a blank canvas. Though the state legislator who authored the first charter law anticipated its being used to expand the sense of ownership and freedom among educators, it was seized upon by others with something else in mind. [21]

Frustrated by the continued inability of districts to improve school quality, parents, educators, and others used chartering to take urban education into their own hands. This can be seen in a number of ways. The first charter law said nothing about closing the achievement gap or expanding the opportunities of disadvantaged students. But as demand shifted, other states put these considerations front and center in their state laws. [22] States with the nation's largest cities are much likelier to have "strong" charter school laws, those supporting charter growth and autonomy. Conversely, many states lacking charter legislation, like Montana, North and South Dakota, Vermont, and West Virginia, lack major urban areas.

But nothing speaks to this point more clearly than the numbers in America's major cities. As of 2010, in Washington, D.C., nearly 40 percent of public school students attend charters. The charter market share is above 30 percent in Dayton and Kansas City, over 25 percent in Gary, St. Louis, and Detroit, and over 20 percent in Albany, Toledo, and Cleveland. [23] More than 25,000 students attend charters in each of the large cities of New York, Los Angeles, and Houston. And in the wake of Hurricane Katrina, New Orleans rebuilt its public education system largely as a network of charter schools. In 2010, more than 60 percent of its public school students were in charters.

THE PURPOSES AND POTENTIAL OF CHARTERING

Although the proliferation of charter schools in cities is arguably the sector's greatest strength, it also highlights a continued weakness in our thinking about this innovative mechanism. Even the most bullish charter proponents have seen only the school-level benefits of chartering.

For example, those who have started charters in disadvantaged communities have sought to provide a higher-performing alternative to a child assigned to a failing district school. Those who've touted charter accountability have argued that the performance contract would focus the attention of the school's adults. Advocates of charter flexibility thought it would liberate a school's teachers. Advocates of autonomy thought it would strengthen the principal.

In fact, a 2005 analysis of the preambles of charter laws found that states had at least eighteen different stated motives for adopting chartering as a reform strategy. Nearly all of them related to activities at the school or classroom level.[24] This thread reaches back to the very first charter law. Reflecting on her work authoring Minnesota's legislation, former state senator Ember Reichgott Junge explained that her ultimate goal was to give teachers more ownership of their schools.[25]

But as chartering developed over the last two decades, it has subtly suggested that it has far more to offer than school-level benefits. The first indications came with the drift away from merely teacher-developed schools. Without this limitation, chartering's blank canvas opened the door to a virtually limitless array of new and different schools run by a wide assortment of individuals and groups.

Next was the creation of non-district authorizers, which removed districts' exclusive authority to operate public K–12 schools, leading to Kolderie's "open sector" of public education. This was enhanced by the lifting of caps on charter school growth. Instead of operating as a constrained, experimental subsidiary to the traditional system, charter schooling's expansion was increasingly allowed to track with market conditions, like community need, parental demand, and educator interest.

Finally, chartering exploded in urban America. It capitalized on the deep frustration with district performance. Instead of leading to a handful of niche schools, it has spawned a new sector within public education.

Considered together, these developments reveal that chartering isn't merely an addition or amendment to the traditional school system; it is a wholly new system of managing public education. One of the first to notice this shift was Ray Budde, the progenitor of the charter school concept. As chartering began to flourish in this unexpected way, Budde expressed misgivings. His intention was to help districts improve by changing the ways that schools were operated. Chartering was instead being used to create new and different types of schools, often outside of districts, leading to some sort of new, parallel system.[26]

What Budde hadn't yet realized, and what too few reformers understand even today, is that improving school systems and creating new and diverse schools are not two different strategies. In fact, the only way to accomplish the former is through the latter.[27] It is important to note, however, that the continuous development of new schools cannot alone drive fundamental improvement in dysfunctional education systems. But when paired with a number of other strategies, it is at the heart of the proper management of a city's portfolio of schools.

A decade ago, the policy world recognized that chartering wasn't just the next in a long line of ballyhooed but short-lived reforms. Its contributions earned Minnesota the prestigious "Innovations in American Government Award" from Harvard's Kennedy School of Government in 2000. More than ten years later, however, it's becoming clearer that these contributions pale in comparison to chartering's potential. In chapter 7, the four systemic innovations of chartering will be explored. These innovations will enable cities to drive continuous improvement in ways the district system simply cannot. These ideas provide the backbone for the central argument in this book: The principles of chartering lie at the heart of the urban school system of the future.

But in chapter 6, we examine the performance of cities' charter sectors for two reasons: first, to make the case for a comprehensive system of education that includes all school sectors; second, to show the remarkable results that are possible when chartering's systemic innovations are thoughtfully and faithfully applied.

NOTES

1. See Diane Ravitch, *The Great School Wars: A History of the New York City Public Schools* (New York: Basic Books, 1988).

2. David Tyack, *The One Best System: The History of American Urban Education* (Boston: Harvard University Press, 1974), 88–97.

3. Diane Ravitch, *Left Back: A Century of Battles over School Reform* (New York: Simon and Schuster, 2001), 20.

4. Ravitch, *Left Back.*

5. Tyack, *The One Best System.*

6. Diane Ravitch and Joseph P. Viteritti, "Introduction," from *New Schools for a New Century: The Redesign of Urban Education* (New Haven, CT: Yale University Press, 1999), 2.

7. See Tables 32 and 87 in Thomas D. Snyder, Sally A. Dillow, and Charlene M. Hoffman, *Digest of Education Statistics 2008* (Washington, DC: National Center for Education Statistics, Institute for Education Sciences, U.S. Department of Education, 2009).

8. From 1950 to 2006, the number of district administrators doubled and "instructional coordinators" grew by nearly a factor of seven. See Table 80 in Snyder, Dillow, and Hoffman, *Digest of Education Statistics 2008.*

9. Ted Kolderie, "The States Will Have to Withdraw the Exclusive," (Minneapolis, MN: Public School Redesign Project, July 1990).

10. See Ray Budde, "The Evolution of the Charter Concept," *Phi Delta Kappan* 78, September 1996, 72–3.

11. Kolderie summarized this plan in Ted Kolderie, "Joe Loftus' 1988 Proposal for 'Charter Schools,'" http://www.educationevolving.org/pdf/JoeLoftus1988CharterProposal.pdf.

12. Joe Nathan, *Charter Public Schools: A Brief History and Preliminary Lessons* (Minneapolis: University of Minnesota, Center for School Change, 1995).

13. "Shanker Asks Greater Autonomy for Teachers and School Officials," *New York Times*, April 1, 1988.

14. Albert Shanker, "Convention Plots New Course—A Charter for Change," *New York Times*, July 10, 1988.

15. Rudy Perpich, "Foreword," and Joe Nathan, "Introduction," in *Public Schools by Choice: Expanding Opportunities for Parents, Students, and Teachers*, ed. Joe Nathan (Bloomington, IN: Meyer Share Books, 1989), 2, 11.

16. Jon Schroeder, *Ripples of Innovation: Chartering Schooling in Minnesota, the Nation's First Charter School State* (Washington, DC: Progressive Policy Institute, April 2004).

17. See Ted Kolderie, "How the Idea of 'Chartering' Schools Came About: What Role Did the Citizens League Play?" *Minnesota Journal* 25, no. 5 (July 2008), 5–6, http://www.citizensleague.org/publications/journal/archives/MNJournalJuly2008.pdf.

18. "Chartered Schools = Choices for Educators + Quality for All Students," Citizens League Policy Report No. 424 (St. Paul, MN: Citizens League, November 1988).

19. See Bryan Hassel and Michelle Godard Terrell, *The Rugged Frontier: A Decade of Public Charter Schools in Arizona* (Washington, DC: Progressive Policy Institute, June 2004); Bryan Hassel, Michelle Goddard Terrell, and Julie Kowal, "Florida Charter Schools: Hot and Humid with Passing Storms" (Washington, DC: Education Sector, 2006).

20. Nelson Smith, "Texas Roundup: Charter Schooling in the Lone Star State" (Washington, DC: Progressive Policy Institute, February 2005), 11.

21. *Chartering 2.0 Leadership Summit Proceedings Document* (Washington, DC: National Alliance for Public Charter Schools, January 2006), 9–10.

22. Andrew Smarick, *Original Intent: What Legislative History Tells Us about the Purposes of Chartering* (Washington, DC: National Alliance for Public Charter Schools, 2005).

23. See "Schools Overview," National Alliance for Public Charter Schools' *Dashboard* Charter School Market Share, http://dashboard.publiccharters.org/dashboard/schools/page/overview/year/2010.

24. Smarick, *Original Intent*.

25. *Chartering 2.0 Leadership Summit Proceedings Document*.

26. Budde, "The Evolution of the Charter Concept," 72–3.

27. Budde came to understand the implications of chartering: "We now have a rapidly expanding charter school movement that is challenging the traditional form of organization of the local school district," in Budde, "The Evolution of the Charter Concept."

Chapter 6

The Charter Quality Curve

Since chartering's inception, the natural question has been, "So, how are charter schools doing?" Though seemingly simple, this question can be approached in many ways, and this has been at the root of years of heated and often unconstructive debate. In fact, the most important questions have gone unanswered nearly twenty years into the sector's existence.

A large part of this confusion is the result of various groups actually asking different questions. Researchers have generally tried to determine, on average, how student performance in charters compares to performance in traditional public schools. They have viewed charter status as akin to a reading program or school uniforms—a characteristic that can be used to differentiate schools. So the common tack has been to group all charters together and compare that category's average achievement level with the average achievement level of non-charter public schools.

Researchers have also investigated the competitive impact of charters, the question being whether charters are forcing district schools to improve. Though a different question than the first, both fail to differentiate between schools within the charter sector. Both treat charter status as the determinative feature of these schools.

A parent searching for the best school for her child, however, is likely to ask a different question. She's almost certainly unconcerned about the health of the entire national charter sector or her state's charter sector. Knowing that schools are made up of countless characteristics, she would evaluate each school individually. She would soon have confirmation of what her intuition whispered at the start—that there is great variation between all of the schools she visits. Charter status alone is as revealing as the number of syllables in the school's name.

This chapter argues that this parent's approach is far more instructive than the common scholarly approach because it exposes critical truths about the charter sector. But even this doesn't fully tell us what we really need to know. Since the true value of chartering lies in its systemic contributions, our focus must shift from the school level to the system level. If we are to understand this mechanism's potential, we need to see "charter"—as Kolderie and Graba have argued—not as an adjective describing a type of school but as a verb indicating how a set of schools are started and assessed.

With this insight, the operative question then becomes, "How well is chartering functioning as a mechanism for managing a portfolio of public schools over time?"

OFF ON THE WRONG TRACK

Since the start of chartering, researchers have used many strategies to assess performance. Some have studied charters in a city, others in a state; some looked nationwide. Many used test scores, others graduation rates. These studies were tracked with varying levels of interest within education circles, but they were little noticed elsewhere.

This changed in 2004 when the *New York Times* reported on findings from the National Assessment of Educational Progress (NAEP). The article began, "The first national comparison of test scores among children in charter schools and regular public schools shows charter school students often doing worse than comparable students in regular public schools."[1]

When statistical controls and other considerations were taken into account, the difference between the two sectors was more equivocal, but still the results demanded attention. They were announced front-page and above-the-fold in the nation's newspaper of record, and they were based on scores from the widely trusted "Nation's Report Card." They reported that, for the most part, there was little difference between traditional public and charter public schools.

The article spawned countless follow-up stories across the country and set off a running volley of alternate analyses and accusations between charter supporters and opponents. The most noticeable upshots from this controversy were increased public awareness about the charter achievement debate and the certainty of new charter analyses following the release of future NAEP results.

But something subtler and ultimately more pernicious had taken root. The approach of the *New York Times* was now understood as the way to evaluate chartering: Average charter scores, average traditional public school scores, compare the results, then declare a winner. The studies on charter performance that preceded this controversy generally took the same form. They also painted a mixed picture; some showed charters in a strong light while others didn't. In combination, all of these findings gave the impression that the charter sector had a performance record roughly equivalent to the traditional public schools sector.

But charter advocates rightly pointed out that NAEP and most other assessments only provide a "snapshot" of student performance at one point in time. If charter schools enroll students with lower incoming achievement rates and more hard-to-quantify disadvantages, such tests would understate the value-added of charter schools. The only assessments that should be considered, advocates argued, are those that measure the performance gains of individual students over time.

Accordingly, in 2005 the National Alliance for Public Charter Schools began publishing a report summarizing all of the major charter achievement studies. Updated frequently to reflect the constantly growing body of research, the report distinguishes between the high-quality value-added studies and the less reliable snapshot studies.[2] Though a slightly higher number of the preferred studies showed a charter advantage, overall, the results, when juxtaposed with the lower-quality studies, were similarly equivocal. Some showed charters on top; some showed traditional public schools on top; and some had mixed results.

In 2009, one education researcher summarized the emerging conventional wisdom: "The people who said this (chartering schooling) was going to be the greatest thing since sliced bread were wrong. The people who said it would be a calamity were equally wrong."[3]

While growth measures represented a methodological advancement for the field, these studies had the same flaw. They too treated the charter sector as a monolith. All reported on the average performance of schools with "charter" in their names. But as chapter 3 showed, there is extraordinary performance variation among similarly impoverished traditional urban public schools. Any discussion of average performance across that sector masks important differences between schools.

The same might apply to the charter sector. If quality varies widely in the highly regulated traditional sector, we ought to expect at least the same in the freer charter sector. So the succinct summary of the research quoted above ought to be tweaked: it's not that chartering is neither the best thing since sliced bread nor a calamity; it's that the range of schools chartering has created could include *both* the best things since sliced bread *and* calamities.

VARIATIONS IN CHARTER PERFORMANCE

A number of individuals and organizations have recognized individual charters for their outstanding achievements. In 2011, fifteen charters were selected for the U.S. Department of Education's "Blue Ribbon Schools Program," an honor bestowed on schools with superior academic performance or
evidence of dramatic student gains. These schools included urban charters in
cities like Oakland, Newark, and Pittsburgh. The Department also released
two reports publicizing the remarkable achievements of some of the nation's
most outstanding charters, most of which were in cities, including Cleveland,
Phoenix, and San Francisco.[4]

Newsweek's 2009 list of the nation's one hundred best high schools included seventeen charters, a number of which were in big cities.[5] A 2006
New York Times Magazine article detailed the outstanding work of three
charter networks operating predominantly in inner-city neighborhoods.[6] A
number of recent popular books such as David Whitman's *Sweating the
Small Stuff* and Jay Mathews' *Work Hard, Be Nice* follow the dazzling work
of urban charters.[7] Some studies have researched the remarkable performance of high-quality charter networks.[8] Oprah Winfrey featured the spectacular work of several charters on her television program, and Microsoft
founder Bill Gates has spoken often about stellar charter schools.[9]

But there's another side of the distribution. It seems like every state and
city has had its share of troubled charters, a reliable pattern uncovered in a
number of case studies. A report on Florida found that in 2005, 26 percent of
charters earned a D or F in the state accountability system. In 2004, six
percent of Arizona's charters received the lowest rating on state achievement
tests.

Slowly research is reporting on the quality differences within the sector.
A 2008 *EducationNext* article discussed the "good deal of variation in
achievement effects" among New York City's charters. It found that 19
percent of the city's charter students attended a school that had "very large"
achievement effects in math relative to traditional public schools, six percent
attended a charter with negative effects, and the rest were spread between
small to moderate (18 percent) and large (56 percent) gains.[10]

More recently, a major study from Stanford University found "wide variation in performance" among the nation's charter schools. Of the more than
2,400 charters studied, nearly half had math gains statistically indistinguishable from traditional public schools; 17 percent of charters had larger gains,
and 37 percent had smaller gains.

Though these results suggest a lagging national charter school sector, the
report emphasized that a "new schools effect" depressed charter scores: more
mature charter schools outperform those in their first year, and students in

their first year at a charter often have smaller gains. Irrespective of the proportion of charter schools at, above, and below the district school mean, the important point is that there is very wide performance variation within the sector.[11]

In 2010, the U.S. Department of Education released a study with remarkably similar findings. Though, on average, the charters studied performed the same as comparison traditional public schools, the study reported "these averages mask variation across the schools in their impacts on students." Some charters led to significant declines in achievement while others greatly increased test scores.[12]

Recently, two leaders with drastically different views of chartering rendered similar conclusions. Nelson Smith, then-president of the national charter advocacy organization, wrote of three groups of charter schools: a high-achieving, path-breaking set; a group at the bottom that are failing their students; and a large group in the middle. "The argument among researchers," said Smith, "is mostly about the size of each tier." Dennis Van Roekel, the president of the National Education Association, which has long been antagonistic to charters, said, "We all know there are some great charter schools. We also know there are some that aren't so good."[13]

CHARTER PERFORMANCE DATA

The same analysis earlier applied to traditional urban public schools is now applied to the charter sectors of several cities. The hypothesis is that, as was the case with schools run by traditional districts, charter quality would be broadly distributed, even when considering only the lowest income schools. Indeed, not only does charter achievement take the familiar bell-shaped form, the breadth of variation is remarkable.

Figure 6.1 shows just two illustrative examples from Los Angeles and Detroit, but the same pattern applies across other elementary grades in reading and math in these cities. In Los Angeles, even when looking only at schools with more than 60 percent of students qualifying for free or reduced-price lunch, 73 percentage points separate the highest- and lowest-performing charters in fourth grade math. The highest-performing school has a poverty rate nearly 10 percentage points higher than the lowest performing school.

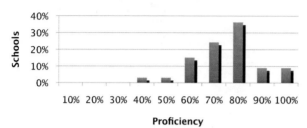

Figure 6.1a

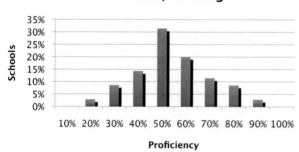

Figure 6.1b

Similarly, in Detroit, 60 percentage points separate the best and worst very low-income charters in fourth grade math and reading. Though two Detroit charters have nearly identical poverty rates (93 percent), one is in the top four in both reading and math while the other is near the bottom in both. The same results are also seen in eighth grade when including another city (Figure 6.2).

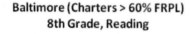

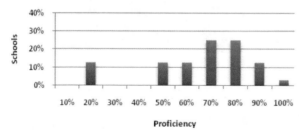

Figure 6.2a

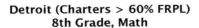
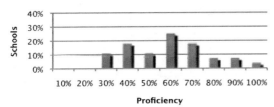

Detroit (Charters > 60% FRPL)
8th Grade, Math

Figure 6.2b

In Baltimore, among the poorest schools, the highest and lowest scores in eighth grade math and reading are separated by 56 and 67 percentage points, respectively. In Detroit, the highest- and lowest-performing schools in eighth grade reading are separated by 79 percentage points (95 percent and 16 percent proficiency). The highest poverty secondary charter in Detroit (98 percent) has the second highest math scores and third highest reading scores in eighth grade.

CHARTER-DISTRICT DISTRIBUTION COMPARISONS

To facilitate comparisons between the charter and district sectors, normal distributions were created using test score means and standard deviations. In a number of cases, the two sectors have similar distributions (comparable means and standard deviations), illustrated by fourth grade scores from Los Angeles and Detroit (Figure 6.3).

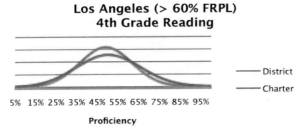

Los Angeles (> 60% FRPL)
4th Grade Reading

Figure 6.3a

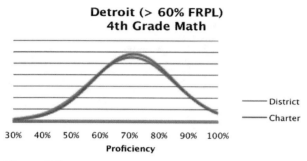

Figure 6.3b

A second finding is that in several cases the mean score for the charter school sector is equal to or higher but its standard deviation is larger, meaning the average low-income charter school is marginally higher performing than its average traditional public school peer, but the variation in performance within the charter sector is wider (Figure 6.4).

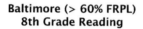

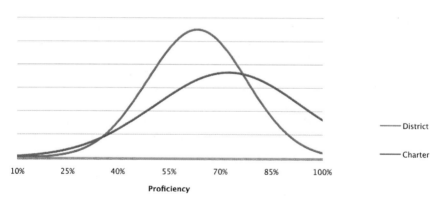

Figure 6.4a

Houston (> 60% FRPL)
8th Grade Math

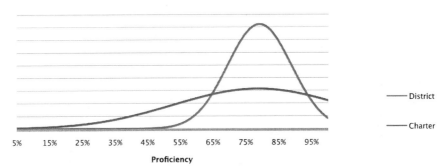

District

Charter

Proficiency

Figure 6.4b

In these cases, the charter sector's broader distribution, as predicted earlier, is the result of its larger number of high-performing and low-performing schools. For example, in eighth grade reading, Baltimore's charter sector has 34 percent of its schools with 80 percent or more proficiency while the traditional public school sector has only 13 percent at this level. But the charter sector also has 25 percent of its schools with only 20 percent to 30 percent of students proficient while the traditional public school sector has no schools performing so lowly.

The great variation in Houston's eighth grade charter scores is also the result of disproportionate numbers of very high and low performers. In math, more than two-thirds of charters have at least 80 percent of their students reaching proficiency, while less than half of traditional public schools hit that mark. But only two percent of traditional public schools have fewer than 50 percent of their students reaching proficiency while 12 percent of charters fall into this category.

But a final finding is the most interesting and most important for our consideration of chartering's systemic potential. The U.S. Department of Education's 2010 study, which spanned fifteen states, found that charters serving the most disadvantaged populations and those in large urban areas had pronounced performance advantages. [14]

A number of recent studies have come to a similar conclusion when looking at specific cities. In big cities where the charter sector is large, the charter policy environment is supportive, and leaders have faithfully executed the charter model, the charter sector is excelling.

Washington, D.C., has had charters for fifteen years, its charter law received an A from the Center for Education Reform, and its charter market share (at 39 percent) is the second largest in the nation. The *Washington Post* found that charters in the nation's capital outperform traditional public schools on both national and state assessments by a wide margin despite serving virtually identical students. [15]

Students in Boston's charter schools were found to have considerably larger achievement gains than students in traditional public schools and pilot schools. [16] Massachusetts has had charters for nearly twenty years, and in 2011 its law was rated as the third strongest in the nation by the National Alliance for Public Charter Schools.

In Philadelphia, 2009 state test results showed that the charter sector had a significant performance advantage over the traditional public school sector. [17] Pennsylvania has had charters for fifteen years, and Philadelphia, with more than forty thousand charter students, has the nation's third largest charter sector.

Similarly positive results can be found in the two cities that have most strongly embraced chartering: New York City and New Orleans. Scholars Caroline Hoxby and Sonali Murarka found that New York City's charters significantly outperform its traditional public schools. [18] The city's low-income charter students were performing nearly as well as students from the city's affluent suburbs. These findings were echoed by Stanford researchers in 2010 who reported that "the typical student in a New York City charter school learns more" than comparable non-charter students. [19]

The same Stanford research team found that New Orleans' charter students were learning significantly more than those in district schools. Consistent with the results above, the researchers found variation in the quality of charters. However, the city has a substantially larger number of high-performing charters (Figure 6.5).

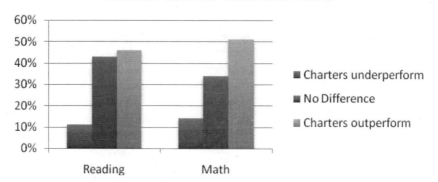

Figure 6.5 Data from Charter School Performance in New Orleans (CREDO, May 2010).

In reading, 46 percent of New Orleans charter schools outperform traditional public schools.

In both subjects, about half of New Orleans' charters significantly outperform comparable traditional public schools and more than a third perform similarly. Only 11 percent (reading) and 14 percent (math) of charters have smaller learning gains.[20]

We have two findings that must be integrated. First, we know there is quality variation in each city's charter sector. Second, in many cities that have significant chartering experience and pursue chartering thoughtfully, the charter sector has, on average, stronger results. Data from New York City offer dramatic graphical evidence of these phenomena. Said simply, New York City's charter sector has successfully shifted the quality curve to the right (Figure 6.6).[21]

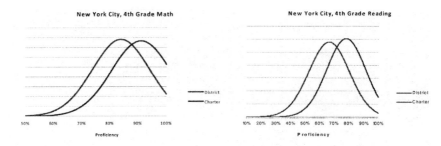

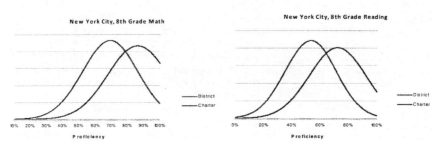

Figure 6.6

In all grades and all subjects analyzed for New York City, the charter sector not only has a higher average score, it also has a nearly identical standard deviation as the traditional public school sector. It has increased average student learning without a concomitant increase in sector-wide variation. In the only instance where the sectors have a significant difference in standard deviation (third grade math), the charter sector has the more consistent results.

In nearly every case, the charter sector has more very high performing schools and fewer low performing schools. In fourth grade reading, 50 percent of charters have at least 80 percent of students proficient, compared to 16 percent of district public schools. In eighth grade math, the charter sector has a 76 percent to 30 percent advantage in the number of schools above 80 percent proficiency. Similarly, charters have fewer schools on the left side of the distribution: In eighth grade reading, nearly half of district schools have proficiency rates under 50 percent; in the charter sector, it's only one in ten.

CONCLUSION

The data presented in this chapter show why discussions of average charter performance are virtually meaningless. Just like the traditional public sector, charters serving very poor student bodies vary in performance.

But when charter performance is compared to traditional public school performance two unavoidable implications are revealed. First, given that the two quality curves are similarly broad and can be found in similar locations on the quality continuum, we'd be wise to develop a sector-blind approach to our cities' schools providers. As we think about how to manage the portfolio to get more schools on the right and fewer on the left, our policies and practices should be geared to each school's performance level, not whether that school is run by a district or charter organization.

But as demonstrated by the positive results in cities that have embraced chartering and the compelling data from New Orleans and New York City in particular, chartering, when done right, has proven itself capable of moving the quality curve to the right. The next chapter focuses on the four systemic innovations of chartering—the explanation behind this success and the building blocks of the urban school system of the future.

NOTES

1. Diana Jean Schemo, "Nation's Charter Schools Lagging Behind, U.S. Test Scores Reveal," *New York Times*, August 17, 2004.
2. Anna Nicotera, *Charter School Achievement: What We Know*, Fifth Edition (Washington, DC: National Alliance of Public Charter Schools, April 2009).
3. Nick Anderson, "Two Charter School Studies, Two Findings on Effectiveness," *Washington Post*, November 30, 2009.

4. U.S. Department of Education, Office of Innovation and Improvement, *K–8 Charter Schools: Closing the Achievement Gap* (Washington, DC: U.S. Department of Education, 2007); Office of Innovation and Improvement, *Charter High Schools: Closing the Achievement Gap* (Washington, DC: U.S. Department of Education, 2006).

5. "Seventeen Public Charter Schools Make Newsweek's List of Top 100 U.S. High Schools," National Alliance for Public Charter Schools, http://dashboard.publiccharters.org/node/960.

6. Paul Tough, "What It Takes to Make a Student," *New York Times Magazine*, November 26, 2006.

7. See David Whitman, *Sweating the Small Stuff: Inner-City Schools and the New Paternalism* (Washington, DC: Thomas B. Fordham Institute, 2008); Paul Tough, *Whatever It Takes: Geoffrey Canada's Quest to Change Harlem and America* (New York: Houghton Mifflin Harcourt, 2008); and Jay Mathews, *Work Hard. Be Nice.: How Two Inspired Teachers Created the Most Promising Schools in America* (Chapel Hill, NC: Algonquin Books, 2009). See also David Whitman, "An Appeal to Authority," *EducationNext* 8, no. 4 (Fall 2008).

8. Katrina R. Woodworth, et al., *San Francisco Bay Area KIPP Schools: A Study of Early Implementation and Achievement. Final Report* (Menlo Park, CA: SRI International, 2008).

9. See for example, "School Solutions," *Oprah.com*, http://www.oprah.com/slideshow/oprahshow/oprahshow1_ss_20060412/1 and Bill Gates, "George Washington University Speech," December 3, 2008, online at http://www.gatesfoundation.org/speeches-commentary/pages/bill-gates-2008-george-washington-university-speech.aspx.

10. Caroline M. Hoxby and Sonali Murarka, "New York City Charter Schools: How Well Are They Teaching Their Students?" *EducationNext* 8, no. 4 (Summer 2008).

11. *Multiple Choice: Charter School Performance in 16 States* (Stanford, CA: Center for Research on Education Outcomes (CREDO), Stanford University, June 2009).

12. Phillip Gleason, et al., *The Evaluation of Charter School Impacts* (Washington, DC: Institute for Education Sciences, U.S. Department of Education, June 2010).

13. Dennis Van Roekel, commenting on Tom Madigan's post, "Do Charter Schools Deserve The Spotlight?," *National Journal Online, Education Experts*, December 7, 2009, http://education.nationaljournal.com/2009/12/do-charter-schools-deserve-the.php.

14. Gleason, et al., *The Evaluation of Charter School Impacts*.

15. Dan Keating and Theola Labbé-DeBose, "Charter Schools Make Gains on Tests," *Washington Post*, December 15, 2008.

16. Atila Abdulkadiroglu, et al., *Informing the Debate: Comparing Boston's Charter, Pilot, and Traditional Schools* (Boston: The Boston Foundation, January 2009). See also Joshua D. Angrist, et al., "Explaining Charter School Effectiveness," Working Paper No. 17332 (Cambridge, MA: National Bureau of Economic Research, August 2011).

17. Martha Woodall, "More City Charter Schools Meet Goals," *Philadelphia Inquirer*, September 4, 2009.

18. Hoxby and Murarka, "New York City Charter Schools."

19. *Charter School Performance in New York City* (Stanford, CA: Center for Research on Education Outcomes (CREDO), Stanford University, January 2010).

20. *Charter School Performance in New Orleans* (Stanford, CA: Center for Research on Education Outcomes (CREDO), Stanford University, May 2010).

21. Stanford researchers found similar results regarding New York City's charters: The sector was higher performing and had less variation overall and fewer low performers than the charter sectors of other cities. See Margaret E. Raymond, "L.A. could learn a lot about charter schools from the Big Apple," *Los Angeles Times*, February 1, 2010, sec. Opinion.

Chapter 7

The Systemic Innovations of Chartering

This book's fundamental argument is that while many urban public schools are deeply troubled, it is the traditional school district that is the problem. This chapter first argues that districts' lack of effective "left-side" and "right-side" strategies and unwillingness to regularly welcome new, diverse entrants into the portfolio explain this field's longstanding struggles. Second, it argues that the four systemic innovations of chartering are perfectly tailored to address these problems. The process through which charter schools are started, monitored, replicated, and held accountable holds the key to successfully managing a portfolio of schools.

STARTING NEW

In healthy industries, new entities constantly enter the fray. Obviously, this process is important in growing markets, when the current batch of providers is unable to generate the quantity of goods or services demanded. But the benefits associated with new starts are expansive.

They can improve the quality of products available, offering the same item but with new features or at a lower cost. They can also introduce new products. Realizing that existing firms are failing to meet the consumer needs, new entrants can develop wholly different offerings. Since customer demands shift regularly, new entrants can help ensure that an industry's products constantly track consumers' preferences. In these ways, new entrants help industries remain high-performing and responsive. Of course, current entities can improve their work and develop new ideas. But the role of new entrants is indispensable for continuous long-term improvement.

As education scholar Frederick Hess has written, "It is hard to point to any field in which systematic measures have produced substantial gains across thousands of entities. More typically, radical and disruptive improvement is the product of new entrants devising a viable product or formula and then creating a coherent organization that faithfully delivers the innovation at scale."[1]

The pioneering work of business scholar Clayton Christensen argues that new entities are responsible for the most important and groundbreaking changes, and older entities typically find themselves unable to sufficiently alter themselves to excel in evolving landscapes.[2]

The power of new entrants can be seen in just about every field. Though dominant for decades, the U.S. auto industry's reputation began declining in the 1970s, opening the door for other carmakers. By early 2009, Toyota had passed the once-invincible General Motors in worldwide car sales, market capitalization, and profitability.[3] In 1995, Google didn't exist; by 2000 it was the world's largest search engine; in 2008, it reported revenues of nearly $22 billion.[4] Though these are famous examples, it's important to keep in mind that the lesson carries across fields. From 2005 to 2008, 22,000 new miscellaneous service firms were started in the United States.[5]

Unfortunately, urban districts' school portfolios generally remained the same year after year. As early as 1967, the Gittell Report on the struggles of New York City's public education cited as primary causes the system's rigidity and "persistent lack of fundamental change."[6] Occasionally a new school might open, but this was typically in response to enrollment growth. A district might start a specialty school for a particular population. But these were exceptions to the rule, and they reflected a desire to address the immediate needs of particular groups not the long-term health of the system.

Chartering brought to an end the era of static school portfolios. Its first contribution was enabling non-district entities to launch public K–12 programs. This was a crucial step toward education's adopting the characteristics of healthy industries.

Importantly though, charter laws did not start any schools; instead, they provided "new organizational space" in which schools could be started. This distinction is critical. Merely starting a batch of schools at a single point in time and then carrying on as before would have badly missed the point. Instead, chartering allowed for a process of continuous new starts so potential entrants would have an unencumbered breezeway into the sector.

Though this was in neither Ray Budde's original thinking nor Minnesota's first law, some early advocates understood this potential. Ted Kolderie wrote of creating "open systems" for new schools as early as 1990.[7] In his first published arguments in favor of chartering, AFT president Albert Shanker lauded the benefits of continuous new starts instead of focusing on accountability or teacher ownership.

He wrote, "The main idea that gripped (AFT convention) delegates was the prospect of having hundreds, even thousands of school teams actively looking for better ways—different methods, technologies, organizations of time and human resources—to produce more learning for more students...The AFT delegates advocated the establishment of a regular policy mechanism that would make innovation an ongoing and valued part of the school community. The idea is to encourage risk-taking and change."[8]

This open space for new schools has two invaluable benefits. First, it allows stellar new offerings to emerge. The outstanding high-poverty, high-performing urban charter schools, like Amistad in New Haven or Citizens Academy in Cleveland, would have never opened were it not for chartering. The second and less-appreciated benefit of open space is that it helps an industry address the lamentable but inevitable fact that not all new starts will succeed. Not every new technology firm catches fire, and not every new clothing line captures the imagination. Some new car models fizzle.

Shanker translated this lesson to education, comparing starting new schools to the journeys of explorer Henry Hudson. Just as there was great potential but "no guarantee" that Hudson would succeed in his mission, there is no guarantee that every new charter school "will find better ways of educating students." But with open space, new starts don't have to be a one-shot opportunity. Instead, they are part of an ongoing process so every unsuccessful entrant can be quickly followed by several others with greater promise.

Some education professionals have a reflexive aversion to admitting that not all schools will succeed. The more comforting approach is arguing that every school, when plied with sufficient good intentions and determination, can be made to excel. This mindset, however, has not only fueled decades of failed improvement efforts (chronicled in chapters 2 and 4), it has also stymied the development of K–12 open space: denying the inevitability of some failure means not needing the bother of new schools.

But other fields have long recognized the compensatory benefits of open space. Popular author Malcolm Gladwell has written about the difficulty of determining in advance which college quarterbacks will succeed in the pros and which business school graduates will excel as financial advisors.[9] Similarly, a leading venture capitalist recently argued, "no good idea that changes the world is universally regarded as one at its outset." He noted that Skype and Hotmail, long before taking off and selling for fortunes, were routinely passed over by investors.[10]

It is instructive that when novice teacher Mike Feinberg launched a fund-raising effort for his first school, all of the city's biggest corporations took a pass, and his friends and family donated only $2,000 combined.[11] It wasn't obvious that Feinberg, a co-founder of KIPP, was starting what would become the nation's most famous network of high-performing, high-poverty schools.

The solution to this unavoidable uncertainty begins by conceding the inevitability of some level of failure—accepting, as Shanker recommended, "a degree of risk"—and then making space for new entrants. Gladwell's metaphor is apt: "Keeping the gate as wide open as possible." (But, of course, this requires tools for properly addressing those that *do* fail, a point to be discussed below.)

Chartering has unlocked the gate of K–12 public education. Since 1992, the chartering mechanism has led to the creation of approximately six thousand new schools. Equally important is the consistency of new starts. In its first years, the national charter sector doubled in size annually, then as the denominator grew, it had several years of 60 percent growth. Once the number of operating charters reached the thousands, several hundred new schools were added each year. Since the 2003–4 school year, the sector has grown at a steady ten percent annual rate.[12]

Consistent growth is occurring in many cities. Since 2005, New York City has opened at least twelve new charters each year (except for the 2007–8 school year when a legislated cap constrained growth). In the fall of 2009, a city record twenty-two new charters opened.[13] In Wayne County, Michigan (Detroit's jurisdiction), the number of charters has grown from ten in 1995–96 to fifty in 1998–99 to ninety-seven in 2010–11.[14] Chicago has opened nine or more charters in each of the last several years.[15] Washington, D.C., which has approximately one hundred charters operating, has consistently opened new schools every year.

Chartering has solved the new entrant problem, demonstrating that new public schools can be developed continuously and in an orderly manner. Moreover, its success has spurred additional "new school strategies" in some urban areas. Both New York City Public Schools and Chicago Public Schools have opened new schools in recent years, the latter through the "Renaissance 2010" initiative, an effort to start one hundred new schools between 2004 and 2010.

Boston began "pilot" schools in 1994 in response to the state's new charter law. Baltimore began the "new school initiative" when the state delayed passing a charter law then started "innovation" schools in 2001 and "transformation" schools in 2008.[16] In the summer of 2009, the Los Angeles Board of Education approved a plan that would allow non-district entities to open fifty new schools.[17]

Chartering could be used in additional ways to start new schools. A state could authorize an already successful nonprofit operator to start an unlimited number of new schools. Quasi-governmental bodies could be established to develop new operators. Or a state could create a new public corporation that would start and operate schools.[18]

Regardless of how chartering evolves in the future, two points are key. First, chartering has already demonstrated that new public schools can be created continuously, which is an essential component of building a healthy public education industry. Second, we have yet to reach the limits of chartering's ability to develop new schools.

DIVERSIFICATION: REMOVING EXCLUSIVE AUTHORITY

The traditional urban school district was designed to own and operate all public schools within a geographic area. Students were assigned to schools based on their home addresses. And because the district was the lone public education delivery system for a century, most assumed that the district and public education were synonymous. Accordingly, for generations, there was entirely too little school diversity within urban public education. But since there are so many different types of students with so many different types of needs and interests, this was a poor formula.

David Tyack summarized the underlying tension as early as 1974, writing, "The search for the one best system has ill-served the pluralistic character of American society."[19] In the years before Minnesota passed its charter law, one of the leaders of that effort wrote, "We believe that true equality of opportunities *demands* that different kinds of programs be available. We think providing identical programs to all students guarantees unequal results."[20]

Of course, a "one-best-system" arrangement would be inconceivable in most other phases of our lives. For our meals, we can choose fast food, sit-down, or carryout, and among each category are countless alternatives. If we prefer to cook at home, we can select from a wide range of grocery and convenience stores, markets, and produce stands. We even have access to specialty outlets like bakeries and delis. The same applies to our housing options. We can rent or buy townhouses, condominiums, apartments, duplexes, and single-family homes. Within each type there are many options—colonial, split-level, split-entry. We can also make choices related to urbanicity, neighborhoods, and builders.

Diversity even abounds in higher education. As of 2007, there were more than 4,300 degree-granting institutions in the United States with more than 1,600 provided by the government, an equal number run by private, nonprofit entities, and more than one thousand operated by for-profit firms.[21] A New Yorker graduating from high school and hoping to stay in state had more than three hundred options.[22] These included sixty-four SUNY campuses, twenty-three CUNY institutions, and numerous private institutions such as Cornell, Syracuse, Columbia, Fordham, Siena, and NYU.

An equivalent array of options was almost entirely absent from urban public schooling until the 1990s. Chartering forever changed that by diversifying the system in two critical ways. Prior to chartering, districts both oversaw and managed schools. Chartering not only separated those functions—into authorization and operation—it expanded the entities able to perform both. Because of chartering, districts now have exclusive authority over neither.

Authorizing

In the early days, state laws often empowered only districts to authorize charter schools. But beginning in 1993, when two states, Michigan and Massachusetts, approved chartering by universities and the state secretary of education, respectively, this all changed. Traditional public school boards lost their "exclusive territorial franchise."

Other states quickly followed. In 1994, Arizona empowered the state board of education and the new Arizona State Board for Charter Schools to approve schools.[23] Other statewide chartering entities soon followed in Washington, D.C., and Colorado.[24] Indiana gave the mayor of Indianapolis the right to authorize schools.[25] Minnesota and Ohio gradually developed increasingly open sectors, allowing universities and nonprofits to authorize.[26]

By 2009, thirty states and Washington, D.C., permitted non-district entities to serve as charter authorizers.[27] Currently, there are five types of non-district authorizers: state education agencies, higher education institutions, nonprofits, municipalities, and independent chartering boards. As of 2012, 957 entities were authorizing charter schools.[28]

This has had a profound systemic impact. Most urban areas today have a public education sector operating outside of the district structure. Half of charter school states allow state education agencies to authorize charters, and more than forty colleges and universities currently oversee charters.

Operators

Minnesota's pioneering 1991 law empowered groups of teachers to run the charter schools in which they worked. Though this shift may have seemed trivial—a small category of individuals could now own and operate a public school—it forever removed districts' claim to being the exclusive provider of public education. Minnesota quickly expanded eligibility beyond certified teachers, and future state laws never included similarly restrictive provisions. The door to diversity was open.

Christensen and his colleagues have written, "Chartering legislation gives innovative educators the tool of separation."[29] This is a fitting description because it reflects the right of different organizations to run public schools and to do so in different ways—different from the traditional district and different from one another.

This separation had two invaluable consequences. First, a disparate array of individuals have committed themselves to starting new public schools. This list includes career educators, lawyers, community organizers, counselors, business executives, professors, and more. Second, the variation in schools opened via chartering is expansive. Michigan's diverse charter sector includes schools that use the Montessori model, schools that adhere to the Core Knowledge curriculum, schools that serve a predominantly Native American population, a school that teaches Armenian culture, and much more.[30]

Minnesota's schools have developed in rural, suburban, and urban communities; many use project-based learning, others make use of online elements. There are schools that serve predominantly Hmong populations; 90 percent of the students at one school are Somali immigrants. There are many schools that aim to serve low-income urban students and others that use Spanish-language immersion.[31]

Chartering has created some of the most innovative schools in America: public boarding schools for inner-city youth, arts-based programs for special needs students, expeditionary learning programs for adjudicated youth. Though charters comprise only five percent of all public schools, they represent 75 percent of the public schools with extended school days and/or school years.[32]

Although successful schools are increasingly identifying their core competencies and then replicating (a subject considered below), the charter world is neither a monolith nor an oligarchy dominated by a few players. Fully 78 percent of charters are "free standing" (or single-site) schools.[33] With such a high proportion unaffiliated with a standard model, diversity continues to define the field.

The diversification of authorizers plays an important role in the diversification of operators. When a single entity has complete control over supply, the list of offerings is all but assured to be limited in variety and numbers. As Henry Ford infamously declared when his company dominated the automobile market: "Any customer can have a car painted any color that he wants so long as it is black."[34] Similarly, the history of chartering has shown that when school districts are a state's only eligible authorizers, that state will have fewer charters and less variation among charters than states with expanded rosters of authorizers.

In total, the ability to start new schools combined with diversification in school authorizers and school operators has generated an entirely new landscape of schools in a growing number of cities (Figure 7.1).

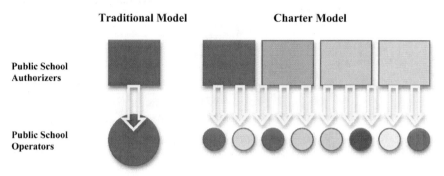

Figure 7.1

In Washington, D.C., for example, ninety-five charter campuses were serving nearly 26,000 students at the end of the 2008–9 school year. This included schools focused on the arts, humanities, technology, special education, law, and more. Seven schools were values-based elementary schools that had once been Catholic schools. There were numerous college-preparatory schools and schools affiliated with higher-education institutions. More than a dozen entities ran more than two schools apiece.

In New Orleans, the flowering of diversification is especially evident. After the storms of 2005, the city's school system was rebuilt largely as networks of charter schools. Now three entities are responsible for overseeing schools: the traditional city school district, a state-authorized "Recovery School District," and the state board of education. While the Recovery School District and the local board of education operate schools, both also oversee charter schools run by others.

About two dozen entities run single schools, while others, including the Algiers Charter Schools Association, KIPP, and the University of New Orleans operate several schools each. In total, in the spring of 2009, there were forty-seven charter schools operated by thirty-two organizations.[35]

But these are just examples of an expanding trend: increasingly robust charter sectors marked by diversity in authorizers and operators are emerging in cities from coast to coast, including Los Angeles, San Francisco, Phoenix, Denver, Houston, Chicago, Detroit, Philadelphia, and New York.

REPLICATIONS AND EXPANSIONS

Possibly the most noticeable feature of a healthy field is the growth of its most successful entities. McDonald's was once a single hamburger stand; Walmart got its start as a five-and-dime; Microsoft started with a single program. In their early, unknown days, they were excellent at what they did. Each could have remained small but instead decided to do more.

Environmental factors contributed to their growth. Their fields didn't erect insurmountable barriers to expansion. There were neither rules barring them from doing more nor an ethic that they ought to be satisfied in their current station. In fact, there were well-known practices and institutions (strategic planning, legal structures, investment capital) that facilitated their growth.

The internal motivation of the leaders of such successful ventures is also key. In the private sector, the primary incentive is assumed to be profit. But other forces come into play. Some want as many people as possible to enjoy their creation. Others want the satisfaction of leading a field. Others like the challenges associated with growth.

Whatever their reasons, countless organizations have decided that expansion makes sense. As a result, the quantity of what great entities produce can be tightly hinged to the public demand. Intel launched its first microprocessor in 1971. By 1994, 85 percent of the world's desktop computers were powered by Intel's chips.[36] Home Depot opened its first store doors in 1979. Twenty-five years later it had nearly two thousand stores, more than three-hundred thousand employees, and annual sales of $73 billion.[37] Netflix launched its subscription service in 1999, and a decade later, it had more than 10 million subscribers.[38]

Growth follows excellence among nonprofits too. Clara Barton and friends started the American Red Cross at the end of the nineteenth century.[39] Today, it has a staff of 35,000, seven hundred local chapters, and a budget over $5 billion.[40] Susan G. Komen for the Cure began in 1982; it has since raised more than a billion dollars to cure breast cancer.[41] Doctors Without Borders, founded in 1971 by a few physicians and journalists, today operates in sixty nations with 27,000 staff and volunteers.[42]

This phenomenon is so sensible and ubiquitous that it seems natural. We see its corollaries everywhere. A great student is encouraged to take more challenging classes. The great defensive coordinator takes over as head coach. A talented salesman is promoted to management. Whether it's Newton or Einstein hatching inspired ideas from humble posts or Oprah Winfrey showing flashes of brilliance as a local news anchor, top performers are allowed, encouraged, and even expected to do more. As Bill Gates has said, "In my experience, when you find a stunning success, you let it grow."[43]

What is so perplexing is that this reasoning was never brought to bear on traditional urban school systems. As shown in chapter 4, high-performing, high-poverty schools are present in cities today. But we never created practices to consistently scale them. Districts lack a "right-side" strategy, a prudent process for dealing with their very best performers. So as a matter of standard operating procedure, each great inner-city school remained an oasis in a vast desert.

Consider the following: Samuel Casey Carters' 2000 book *No Excuses* described the accomplishments of twenty-one high-performing, high-poverty schools. Included were fourteen traditional urban public schools, thirteen of which were still operating in 2009. At the time of the book's release, these thirteen schools combined served 9,020 students across ninety-four grades. In 2009, they served 7,669 students (a drop of 15 percent) across one hundred grades (an increase of four percent). Despite their shocking success and public fame, these schools actually served *fewer* students a decade later. Eight had the same grade spans; four had grown by one grade level, and another by two grade levels.[44] Why in the world weren't these astonishing successes grown?

There are several explanations for why systematic expansions and replications never took place. First, the traditional geography-based student assignment system obscured the possibilities. Since each residential area was thought to need only one school per grade span, to many, replication absent enrollment growth would have seemed illogical. Second, districts may have thought that they did have a right-side strategy: spread success by strategically moving an excelling school's human capital. A great principal could be promoted to a central office job; her assistant principal could take the helm at another school.

Finally, some district leaders might have considered replication and expansion unseemly, the equivalent of turning public education into a commodity. Moreover, since these strategies wouldn't generate additional money, some may have argued that there would be no incentive for anyone to take on this work.

Chartering, however, has brought replications and expansions to public education, enabling some of America's highest performing urban schools to do more. The most famous example comes from the KIPP Foundation. In 1994, two novice teachers, Mike Feinberg and Dave Levin, began the "Knowledge is Power Program" for fifth graders in a Houston public school.

Eventually, Feinberg grew that program into a charter, and Levin started a similar charter in New York City. Both schools had phenomenal success. With philanthropic support, they created a nonprofit designed to scale their model so more students could be served. The result was the KIPP Foundation, which trains educators to start and lead similar schools. As of 2012, the KIPP network serves 32,000 students in 109 schools spread across twenty states and Washington, D.C.

Other organizations have followed suit.[45] In 2003, the leaders of New Haven's exceptional Amistad Academy launched Achievement First, a non-profit "with the express mission of using Amistad's knowledge and best practices to effect dramatic, large-scale student achievement gains in our nation's lowest-performing school districts." As of 2012, it was operating twenty schools in New York and Connecticut. Aspire, the nation's very first replication effort, began with University Public School in 1999 and now runs thirty-four schools in California. Uncommon Schools began with North Star Academy in Newark and now manages twenty-eight superb schools.

These replication-and-support organizations have come to be known as "Charter Management Organizations," or CMOs. CMOs are much smaller than urban school districts; more than 90 percent manage thirty or fewer schools.[46] (By comparison, the average number of schools in the one hundred largest districts is 169.[47]) "Education Management Organizations" (EMOs) are CMOs' for-profit counterparts. In nearly all states, charter laws require that a nonprofit hold the contract with the school's authorizer, so EMOs play a slightly different role.

Typically an EMO is hired to provide services, ranging from payroll and technology assistance to total day-to-day school management. Major national EMOs include Edison Schools (working with thirty-one charter schools), Mosaica Education (thirty-six), and National Heritage Academies (fifty-five).[48]

CMOs and EMOs have become important players in the charter sector, demonstrating the possibilities of replications and expansions. During the 2008–9 school year, CMOs operated more than 550 schools, 12 percent of all charters (up from only three hundred in 2005).[49] EMOs operated nearly five hundred schools, or about ten percent.

In some states, these organizations play a leading role. In Arizona, Michigan, Missouri, and Ohio, EMOs operate at least 20 percent of charter schools; in Connecticut, Illinois, Indiana, New York, Ohio, Texas, and the District of Columbia, CMOs operate at least 20 percent of charters.

Though EMOs are at least partially profit-driven, CMOs have demonstrated that profit is not required to have great models grow. Indeed, many are investing in this work with absolutely no expectation of financial gain. Individual benefactors and philanthropies, like the Walton Family Foundation, the Donald and Doris Fisher Fund, and the Broad Foundation, have provided substantial support to charter expansions and replications. The Bill and Melinda Gates Foundation announced in 2009 an $18.5 million national investment in CMOs.[50]

Others have invested in discrete projects. The Michael and Susan Dell Foundation and the Weingart Foundation have contributed to Green Dot, the Los Angeles-based CMO.[51] Credit Suisse and the Houston Endowment have invested in Texas CMO YES Prep Public Schools.[52]

So important is the work of growing superb charters that two organizations were created with this specifically in mind. NewSchools Venture Fund, founded in 1998, helps educational entrepreneurs scale organizations. It has invested in many of the nation's leading CMOs, including Achievement First, Aspire Public Schools, D.C. Prep, and High Tech High.[53] Launched in 2005 to help grow highly successful charters, the Charter School Growth Fund operates with $150 million in three pools of capital. Its investment portfolio includes IDEA Public Schools, KIPP D.C., and the Noble Network.[54]

Though the replication and expansion of successful schools was made possible by chartering and appears particularly well suited for this sector, its principles have been embraced by a few districts. Former New York City schools chancellor Joel Klein spoke of creating a "Silicon Valley" of education in the Big Apple. He helped recruit high-performing CMOs to start and replicate schools in the city. In a 2009 planning document, Baltimore's district included among its guiding principles the expansion of successful schools.[55]

Chicago Public Schools fostered the replication of several high-performing schools. Boston's superintendent introduced a five-year strategic plan in 2009, and one of four "key strategies" was replicating successful schools.[56]

The replication and expansion of great charter schools is exciting because it enables more students to attend excellent schools. The bigger lesson, however, is that the "right-side" strategy long pursued by other industries but long ignored by traditional urban districts can be successfully applied to urban public schooling.

CLOSURES

The fourth major systemic innovation introduced to public education by chartering is the regular closure of persistently underperforming schools. As discussed in chapter 4, districts have relentlessly attempted to fix their most troubled schools. This has not worked; virtually all failing schools continue to struggle despite interventions.

The experience of other industries demonstrates that public education is not unique in its inability to turn around failures. Consequently, when improvement efforts fail, these other industries have mechanisms for ridding themselves of these entities. And this happens regularly. A market research report found that among the one-hundred-thousand miscellaneous service firms operating in the United States in 2006, only about 75,000 remained two years later.[57]

The stellar book *Creative Destruction*, which tracked shifts in industries, found the same pattern. The authors followed 1,008 companies existing in 1962; by 1996, only 160 remained.[58] Of the five hundred companies originally listed in the S&P 500 in 1957 only seventy-four were left in 1997.[59] This even occurs among the most powerful firms. Of the thirty stocks included on the Dow Jones Index (made up of the nation's largest and most widely held public companies) in the spring of 1959, only seven were still listed in June 2009.

A number of those once-colossal companies, including Bethlehem Steel and Woolworth's, are now defunct. Many others were dismantled and sold.[60] Of the one hundred companies first included on the Forbes list of America largest firms, sixty-one had ceased to exist seventy years later.[61]

Such turnover is also part of our political system. The Twenty-second Amendment, which bars a president from being elected more than twice, guarantees churn in the nation's highest office. Similarly, thirty-eight states prohibit a governor from serving more than two consecutive terms. Fifteen states place limits on the number of terms their state legislators may serve.

Elections serve the same purpose. They enable voters to replace low-performing—as determined by the electorate—incumbents. Every election cycle leads to the end of some number of sitting officials' careers. Occasionally, when the public believes a wholesale change is in order, vast numbers of incumbents are removed. Sitting presidents in 1932 and 1980 were turned out in landslides along with scores of their party colleagues in Congress. More recently, the mid-term elections of 1994, 2006, and 2010 drastically altered the party control in Congress.

It's not that schools never close. But closures have historically been the result of enrollment declines, not conscious quality control. In the nation's capital the majority of traditional public schools selected for closure since 2002 were *not* in the bottom performance quartile.[62] Without question, enrollment-driven closures have been too slow and too few. Many urban districts maintain numerous buildings well below capacity. But even if they managed their stock of facilities to accurately reflect their student enrollment, more would be needed. A full school isn't the same thing as a great school.

In the private sector, a firm's production level is a somewhat reliable proxy for its quality; an extremely busy business is probably better than one routinely without customers. But that relationship doesn't necessarily apply to traditional urban public schools. Because they are populated by geographic zones, a crowded school can be of poor quality and a sparsely enrolled school can be excellent. A mechanism is needed in urban public education to get rid of chronically failing schools, not just under-enrolled schools.

Chartering has shown how this can be done. Charter schools are built on a simple trade: freedom for accountability. An organization is allowed to open an autonomous public school and, in exchange, commits to accomplish explicit goals. The terms of this agreement are spelled out in a performance contract. If that school fails to live up to its end of the bargain, it can be closed.

This small, transparent, and reasonable mechanism has provided something long missing from urban public education: the link between a school's lifespan and its performance. Studies of chartering in various states have shed light on how this process has worked. A report on Minnesota's first twelve years of chartering found that 16 percent of its charters had been closed.[63] The same closure rate was found in Washington, D.C., after its first decade.[64]

Because schools are like other organizations in many ways, "performance" extends beyond academic measures into operational matters. Accordingly, a significant number of charters have been closed for non-academic reasons. By 2006, more than sixty charters in Florida had been closed (about 15 percent), many for financial, governance, or enrollment reasons.[65]

A study of Michigan found that ten percent of its charters had been closed, some for facilities or financial issues.[66] Some Arizona charters were closed for management lapses.[67] National data track with these state-level findings. According to the Center for Education Reform, the national closure rate as of 2009 stood at approximately 13 percent. About two-thirds were for either management or financial reasons.[68]

Some critics have charged that too few low-performing charters have been shuttered, questioning the closure plank of the charter model. One *Washington Post* reporter wrote that President Obama needed to become "the Terminator" of failing charters.[69] Such critics often point to the data presented above showing that substantial number of closures are for non-academic reasons. Two responses to that claim are appropriate.

First, seldom is a school closed for one reason. A 2005 study found, "As a rule, authorizers say schools that are failing academically are generally experiencing problems in other operational areas as well."[70] Typically, one area of weakness causes problems in others.

A school may have been officially closed for financial issues, but these problems were likely precipitated by academic weaknesses, which caused enrollment declines, which led to decreased revenue. So the officially listed cause of closure doesn't necessarily reflect the full contours of the school's story. As one charter school authorizer noted, "They got Al Capone on his taxes."[71]

Second, even if it were true that too many low-performing charters avoid closure, it wouldn't call into question the value of closures to system-wide health. If a diabetic who fails to take insulin as prescribed becomes ill, that doesn't raise suspicions about insulin's efficacy; it merely underscores the importance of implementing the intervention faithfully.

If academic-based closures are too rare, closures as a strategy shouldn't be jettisoned; instead, charter contracts need to be better enforced. The conscientious work of a great number of charter authorizers attests to the ability to close failing schools and its beneficial consequences for the sector.

The closure of failing schools after attempts at improvement has helped the sector address its "left-side" problems. Poor-performing schools go away, contributing to the strong results of the several experienced charter cities highlighted in the previous chapter. It also has important secondary effects. The threat of closure incentivizes existing schools to improve, and when closures do occur, they make room for new schools and the expansion of high-performing schools.

This churning process enables the city's universe of schools to track the varied and changing demands of families. As Paul Hill and his colleagues have written about the tough accountability principles embedded in the portfolio concept, "Schools' existence and freedom of action are contingent on performance, so that every school is under pressure to improve and the district as a whole is constantly searching for a mix of schools that will better meet the needs of the city's population."[72]

Because of these virtues, this process has been embraced by a few reform-oriented urban districts. Joel Klein closed more than one hundred persistently underperforming district schools. Explaining one round of closures, John White, then a Klein deputy and now Louisiana's state superintendent, said, "This proposal is a reflection of our belief that in some schools there is simply not the capacity to fulfill our promise to kids to prepare them for the future."[73] A major research study in 2012 validated New York City's approach: It found that new, small high schools that replaced high schools that were closed had large positive impacts on graduation rates and college readiness.[74]

In 2008, Washington, D.C., chancellor Michelle Rhee, approaching a round of closures, placed a greater emphasis on performance than enrollment, saying, "Academic achievement takes precedence."[75] Plans in Baltimore explicitly call for "closing schools that don't work for our kids."[76] In 2009, Boston's superintendent planned to close as many as a dozen of her district's lowest performing schools.[77] Philadelphia's "Imagine 2014" plan envisioned closing up to thirty-five chronically underperforming district schools.[78]

As the head of public schools in Chicago, Arne Duncan closed sixty-one schools through the Renaissance 2010 initiative.[79] Describing Duncan's grand strategy, a national columnist wrote, "By closing failing schools and opening replacements, Chicago is ensuring that the portfolio of schools is churned and improved."[80]

There is reason for encouragement. In Denver, the closure of eight schools led to improved academic performance by the two thousand students affected.[81] A 2009 Chicago study found that students displaced by closures learned more if they moved into higher-performing schools.[82] The following year, Chicago schools CEO took steps to ensure that all students affected by closures had access to higher-performing options.[83]

As U.S. Secretary of Education, Duncan has called for the closure of low-performing charters, and his department has encouraged states to use a number of federal programs in broader school closure strategies.[84] A number of reform leaders joined forces to support this direction, arguing that, "By 2012 states and districts should have shut down at least five hundred of these (the nation's poorest-performing) schools...(and) every state will have a clear mechanism that it is using to aggressively close its lowest-performing five percent of schools."[85]

Closing schools, even low-performing schools, is difficult work. This can be seen in the public protests when closures are announced, in the hesitancy of some authorizers to shutter struggling schools, and in the lawsuits filed when they do. It has been said that closing a school is as popular as moving a graveyard.[86]

But these implementation challenges shouldn't be confused with the efficacy of the underlying principle—that persistently failing schools ought to be closed for the sake of the children assigned to them and the good of the broader system. Chartering has demonstrated that the logic of closures can be brought to bear on public education.

Although many see autonomy and accountability as the heart of the charter concept, this chapter has argued that its potential is far greater. The four systemic innovations of chartering—new starts, diversification, replications/expansions, and closures—are perfectly suited to address the systemic shortcomings of urban districts.

Implemented fully and properly, these innovations can lead to the development of dynamic, responsive, and self-improving school systems in America's cities. Creating a playbook for operationalizing this vision is the goal of the final section of this book. First, however, attention turns to the third and final sector in urban K–12 education, private schools.

This third section argues that the private schools sector should be integrated into a coherent, comprehensive system of schools with the two other sectors. It is to this grand collection of schools—the city's portfolio—that the principles of chartering ought to be applied.

NOTES

1. Frederick M. Hess, "The Supply Side of School Reform," *Phi Delta Kappan* 90, no. 3, 211–7.
2. For example, see Clayton M. Christensen, *The Innovator's Dilemma : The Revolutionary Book that Will Change the Way You Do Business* (New York: HarperCollins, 2003).
3. "Toyota Passes GM as World's Largest Automaker," *U.S. News and World Report,* January 21, 2009.
4. See *Google,* "Our History in Depth," http://www.google.com/corporate/history.html ; and *Google,* "Financial Information: Financial Tables," http://investor.google.com/fin_data. html.
5. "U.S. Market Research Report: Services, misc." BizMiner, July 2009, http://www.bizminer.com/resources/.
6. Marilyn Gittell, *Participants and Participation* (New York: Praeger, 1967), quoted in Ravitch, *The Great School Wars,* 330.
7. Ted Kolderie, "The States Will Have to Withdraw the Exclusive," (Minneapolis, MN: Public School Redesign Project, July 1990).
8. "Shanker Asks Greater Autonomy for Teachers and School Officials," *New York Times,* April 1, 1988.
9. Malcolm Gladwell, "Most Likely to Succeed," *The New Yorker,* December 15, 2008.
10. Scott Austin, "The Importance of 'Crazy Ideas' To A Successful VC Firm," *Wall Street Journal,* October 9, 2009.
11. Jay Mathews, *Work Hard. Be Nice.: How Two Inspired Teachers Created the Most Promising Schools in America* (Chapel Hill, NC: Algonquin Books, 2009), 91.
12. Jeanne Allen, Alison Consoletti, and Kara Kerwin, *The Accountability Report, 2009: Charter Schools* (Washington, DC: Center for Education Reform, 2009); also "Schools Overview," National Alliance for Public Charter Schools' *Dashboard,* Charter School Market Share, http://dashboard.publiccharters.org/dashboard/schools/page/overview/year/2009.
13. "Charter Schools in New York State," New York Charter Schools Association, http://nycsa.org/Docs/CharterSchoolChart8_25_11.pdf.
14. "Districts and PSAs," Wayne County Regional Educational Service Agency, http://www.resa.net/aboutus/districts/.
15. Chicago Public Schools, "Renaissance 2010: Who We Are," http://cps.edu/NewSchools/Pages/WhoWeAre.aspx , last updated April 20, 2012.
16. See Baltimore City Public Schools, "Charter, Innovation, and Transformation Schools," http://www.baltimorecityschools.org/domain/97 .
17. Associated Press, "LA School Board OKs School Choice Plan with Private Operators," *USA Today,* August 26, 2009.
18. See Ted Kolderie, *Creating the Capacity for Change: How and Why Legislatures are Opening a New-Schools Sector in Public Education* (Bethesda, MD: Education Week Press, 2004) 87–90.
19. David Tyack, *The One Best System: A History of American Urban Education* (Cambridge: Harvard University Press, 1974) 88–97.
20. Joe Nathan, ed. *Public Schools by Choice: Expanding Opportunities for Parents, Students, and Teachers* (New York: HarperCollins, 1989).
21. See Table 230 in Snyder, Dillow, and Hoffman, *Digest of Education Statistics 2008* (Washington, DC: U.S. Department of Education, March 2009).
22. See Table 271, Degree-Granting Institutions, Number and Enrollment by State: 2005," in U.S. Census Bureau, *Statistical Abstract of the United States: 2009* (Washington, DC: Government Printing Office, 2008).
23. See Hassel and Terrell, *The Rugged Frontier: A Decade of Charter Schooling in Arizona* (Washington, DC: Progressive Policy Institute, 2004).

24. See Mead, *Capital Campaign: Early Returns on District of Columbia Charters* (Washington, DC: Progressive Policy Institute, 2005); and Todd Ziebarth, *Peaks & Valleys: Colorado's Charter School Landscape* (Washington, DC: Progressive Policy Institute, December 2005).

25. Bryan C. Hassel, *Fast Break in Indianapolis: A New Approach to Charter Schooling* (Washington, DC: Progressive Policy Institute, September 2004).

26. Jon Schroeder, *Ripples of Innovation: Charter Schooling in Minnesota, the Nation's First Charter School State*; and Alexander Russo, *A Tough Nut to Crack in Ohio: Charter Schooling in the Buckeye State* (Washington, DC: Progressive Policy Institute, February 2005).

27. "An Overview of Non-District Authorizers" (Washington, DC: National Alliance for Public Charter Schools, March 2009).

28. Sean Conlon and Alex Medler, *The State of Charter School Authorizing 2011: Fourth Annual Report on NACSA's Authorizer Survey* (Chicago: National Association of Charter School Authorizers, January 2012), 4.

29. Christensen, Hern, and Johnson, *Disrupting Class: How Disruptive Innovation Will Change the Way the World Learns* (New York: McGraw Hill, 2008), 209.

30. Sara Mead, "Maintenance Required: Charter Schooling in Michigan," *Education Sector*, October 19, 2006, 10; also Mead, *Capital Campaign*.

31. Schroeder, *Ripples of Innovation.*

32. David A. Farbman, *Tracking An Emerging Movement: A Report on Expanded-Time Schools in America* (Boston: National Center on Time and Learning, December 2009).

33. Schools by Management Organization 2008–09, National Alliance for Public Charter Schools, Public Charter School *Dashboard*, http://www.publiccharters.org/dashboard/schools/page/mgmt/year/2009 .

34. Henry Ford with Samuel Crowther, *My Life and Work* (Garden City, NY: Garden City Publishing, 1922), 72.

35. "New Orleans Schools Governance Structure, 2008–09" (New Orleans: The Scott S. Cowen Institute for Public Education Initiatives at Tulane University, March 2009).

36. "Corporate Timeline: A History of Innovation," Intel Corporation, http://www.intel.com/museum/corporatetimeline/index.htm?iid=intel_info+rhc_history.

37. "Our Company, The History and Interactive Timeline," Home Depot, http://corporate.homedepot.com/wps/portal/!ut/p/c1/04_SB8K8xLLM9MSSzPy8xBz9CP0os3gDdwNHH0sfE3M3AzMPJ8MAF0sDKND388jPTdUvyHZUBAB6afqn/dl2/d1/L2dJQSEvUUt3QS9ZQnB3LzZfMEcwQUw5TDQ3RjA2SEIxUEY5MDAwMDAwMDA!/..

38. "About Netflix," Netflix: Press Kit, http://www.netflix.com/MediaCenter?id=5379#about.

39. "About Us, Red Cross History," American Red Cross, http://www.redcross.org/portal/site/en/menuitem.86f46a12f382290517a8f210b80f78a0/?vgnextoid=271a2aebdaadb110VgnVCM10000089f0870aRCRD .

40. "About Us, Red Cross History;" and "The 200 Largest US Charities, The American Red Cross," Forbes, http://www.forbes.com/lists/2007/14/pf_07charities_American-Red-Cross_CH0013.html.

41. "About Us," Susan G. Komen for the Cure, http://ww5.komen.org/AboutUs/AboutUs.html.

42. "About Us, History and Principles," Doctors Without Borders, http://doctorswithoutborders.org/aboutus/?ref=main-menu.

43. "Bill Gates's speech to the National Conference of State Legislatures (July 21, 2009)," Bill and Melinda Gates Foundation, http://www.gatesfoundation.org/speeches-commentary/Pages/bill-gates-2009-conference-state-legislatures.aspx.

44. Samuel Casey Carter, *No Excuses: Lessons from 21 High-Performing, High-Poverty Schools* (Washington, DC: The Heritage Foundation, 2000). Enrollment and grade span data for 2009 collected from school and district websites and the now-defunct schoolmatters.com .

45. See Joanna Smith, et al., "Mapping the Landscape of Charter Management Organizations" (paper presented at the Annual Meeting of the American Educational Research Association, San Diego, CA April 13–17, 2009).

46. Smith, "Mapping the Landscape of Charter Management Organizations."

47. Jennifer Sable, Chris Plotts, and Lindsey Mitchell, *Characteristics of the 100 Largest Public Elementary and Secondary School Districts in the United States: 2008–09 (NCES 2011-301)*. U.S. Department of Education, National Center for Education Statistics (Washington, DC: U.S. Government Printing Office, 2010).

48. For more on EMOs, see Alex Molnar, Gary Miron, and Jessica Urschel, *Profiles of For-Profit Educational Management Organizations: Tenth Annual Report* (Boulder: Education and the Public Interest Center, University of Colorado, July 2008).

49. National Alliance for Public Charter Schools, *Public Charter Schools Dashboard*, "Schools by Management Organization: 2008–09 National," http://www.publiccharters.org/dashboard/schools/page/mgmt/year/2009.

50. Smith, "Mapping the Landscape of Charter Management Organizations."

51. See Green Dot Public Schools: Our Supporters, http://www.greendot.org/page.cfm?p=1664.

52. YES Prep Public Schools: Our Supporters, http://yesprep.org/SupportYES/topic/our_supporters/.

53. NewSchools Venture Fund: Our Ventures, http://www.newschools.org/portfolio/ventures.

54. Charter School Growth Fund: Portfolio Members, http://www.chartergrowthfund.org/?q=node/28.

55. Baltimore City Public Schools, *Expanding Great Options SY 2010: Reviewing Schools to Maximize Success for Students*, April 2009.

56. Boston Public Schools, *Acceleration Agenda 2009–2014: A Five-Year Strategic Direction to Transform the Boston Public Schools*, November 18, 2009.

57. "U.S. Market Research Report."

58. Foster and Kaplan, *Creative Destruction.*

59. Quoted in Joe Graba, "We Cannot Get the Schools We Need by Changing the Schools We Have."

60. Dow Jones Indexes: Dow Jones Industrial Average, Historical Components, http://www.djindexes.com/mdsidx/downloads/DJIA_Hist_Comp.pdf.

61. Richard Foster and Sarah Kaplan, *Creative Destruction: Why Companies That Are Built to Last Underperform the Market—And How to Successfully Transform Them* (New York: Doubleday, 2001).

62. "Public Charter School and DCPS School Closings Since 2002," FOCUS, April 2009.

63. Schroder, *Ripples of Innovation.*

64. Mead, *Capital Campaign.*

65. Bryan Hassel, Michelle Goddard Terrell, and Julie Kowal, "Florida Charter Schools: Hot and Humid with Passing Storms" (Washington, DC: Education Sector, 2006).

66. Sara Mead, *Maintenance Required: Charter Schooling in Michigan* (Washington, DC: Education Sector, October 2006).

67. Hassel and Terrell, *The Rugged Frontier.*

68. Allen, Consoletti, and Kerwin, *The Accountability Report 2009.*

69. Jay Mathews, "Mr. President: Be the Bad Guy, Start Closing Schools," *Washington Post*, December 1, 2009.

70. Andrew Rotherham, "The Pros and Cons of Charter School Closures," in *Hopes, Fears, and Realities: A Balanced Look at American Charter Schools in 2005*, eds. Robin J. Lake and Paul T. Hill (Seattle: National Charter School Research Project, Center on Reinventing Public Education, Daniel J. Evans School of Public Affairs, University of Washington, 2005), 43–52.

71. Jim Goenner, head of the Central Michigan University charter schools office, quoted in Rotherham, "The Pros and Cons of Charter School Closures."

72. Paul Hill, et al., *Portfolio School Districts for Big Cities: An Interim Report* (Seattle, WA: Center on Reinventing Public Education, October 2009).

73. Sharon Otterman, "City to Shut 4 Schools for Poor Performance; More Closings Expected," *New York Times*, December 2, 2009, sec. New York Region.

74. Howard S. Bloom and Rebecca Unterman, *Sustained Positive Effects on Graduation Rates Produced by New York City's Small Public High Schools of Choice* (New York: MDRC, January 2012).

75. V. Dion Haynes, "Parents Protest Plan for School Closures," *Washington Post,* February 28, 2008.

76. Baltimore City Public Schools, *Expanding Great Options SY2010.*

77. Edward Mason, "Schools Told To Shape Up or They'll Be Closed," *Boston Herald,* November 18, 2009.

78. Kristen A. Graham, "School Changes Won't Be Forced, Ackerman Says," *Philadelphia Inquirer*, August 21, 2009.

79. In one of his final actions before taking over as U.S. Secretary of Education, Duncan called for the closure or consolidation of twenty-five underperforming or under-enrolled schools. Maudlyne Ihejirika and Cheryl Jackson, "25 Schools Set for Shakeup," *Chicago Sun-Times*, January 11, 2009; see also, Amanda Paulson, "Chicago Hope: 'Maybe This Will Work,'" *Christian Science Monitor*, September 21, 2004.

80. George Will, "Calling the Baby Ugly," *Newsweek,* March 23, 2009.

81. Jeremy P. Meyer, "'07 School Closings Boost Student Achievement, DPS Analysis Finds," *The Denver Post*, September 24, 2009.

82. Marisa de la Torre and Julia Gwynne, *When Schools Close: Effects on Displaced Students in Chicago Public Schools* (Chicago IL: Consortium on Chicago School Research, October 2009).

83. "Student Learning Plans, Improving School Culture Will Be Part of this Year's School Turnarounds," Catalyst Chicago, *Catalyst Notebook*, January 19, 2010.

84. "American Recovery and Reinvestment Act of 2009 : Using ARRA Funds to Drive School Reform and Improvement," U.S. Department of Education, April 24, 2009; and U.S. Department of Education, "Notice of Proposed Priorities: Race to the Top Fund," in *Federal Register* 74, no. 144, July 29, 2009.

85. *Smart Options: Investing the Recovery Funds for Student Success*, Coalition for Student Achievement, April 2009, http://broadeducation.org/asset/429-arrasmartoptions.pdf.

86. Rotherham, "The Pros and Cons of Charter School Closures."

Part III

Urban Private Schooling

Typically, in discussions of urban education reform, private schools are an afterthought. Virtually the entire focus is on the traditional public school district and, increasingly, the charter public school sector.

To the extent that private schools are included, the conversation turns directly to vouchers or tuition tax credits, avenues into private schools for low-income children that nevertheless keep private schools separated from their public counterparts. Indeed, practically all of our public policies preserve the pretense that public education and private education are separate enterprises.

But they are similar in most material ways. All schools need educators and supplies. They must manage facilities, payrolls, and vendors. They are critical parts of their neighborhoods, and they have deep responsibilities to families, namely a shared mission to prepare young people for lifetime success. And in the case of urban education, another similarity is critically important: Urban private schools—particularly faith-based urban private schools—serve many low-income students.

Years ago, it could have been argued that the major difference between private schools and traditional public schools—that the former were run by non-district entities—required that the two sectors be treated differently. But charters are run by a vast collection of organizations and yet they are still fully part of the public education system. In fact, other differences of private education, such as its use of specialized curricula and non-certified teachers, are also seen in charter public schools. Moreover, nearly all of our closest international peers have built policies that treat their government-run and privately operated schools similarly. So we know that the distinctions we've drawn aren't prevalent, much less necessary.

The point is that maybe our old lines need reconsidering. As we contemplate how best to craft a sensible system for managing urban K–12 education, it might be neither required nor wise to exclude private schools from the conversation. This section argues that private schools should be included in the discussion to a far greater extent than before. This case will be made in several ways, including through comparisons to other nations and a discussion of the ongoing closures of America's urban faith-based schools. But two reasons—one philosophical and one practical—are worth noting in advance.

First, while our focus has been on school systems and often the unit of analysis has been schools, the ultimate concern is the fate of children. Therefore, the central issue is what types of schools and systems of schools best serve needy kids. Unfortunately, too many have begun the conversation with a different question, something along the lines of, "How can we improve the traditional system of public education?" or "How can we improve our public schools?"

Such a framework, of course, is limiting and unnecessarily so as conceived here. The straightforward goal is to get urban students (*all* urban students) in great schools (*all* great schools). Said another way, this book is rooted in a firm agnosticism about school sector. We should be indifferent to who operates a school so long as that school is safe and rigorous, meets the needs of students, and adheres to democratic, pluralistic principles. In the eyes of this study, school quality is exponentially more important than school provider.

This book's nearly single-minded focus on quality has been revealed in a number of ways in previous chapters. The two public sectors were subjected to the same analysis—a search for the quality distribution among similarly impoverished schools. Additionally, it has been argued that the determining factor for how a school should be treated by policy was where it stood along the quality continuum, not the sector to which it belonged.

The second reason private schools are paid greater attention in this study relates to the central findings teased out earlier. The case has been made that our urban public education policies reflect a deeply flawed strategy for failing schools, no strategy for highly successful schools, and insufficient attention to the importance and characteristics of new schools. It was argued that the four innovations of chartering could help solve these problems and lead to a dynamic, responsive, high-performing, and self-improving urban education system.

But those innovations could also be applied to the private schools sector. Though some adjustments would be required, their application could help shrink the number of low-quality seats and generate more high-quality seats over time, contributing greatly to the overall quality of the portfolio.

Explaining how to translate these innovations into a policy framework is the concern of the final section of this book. First, we take a look at the development and status of America's urban private schools, how they currently fit into the broader K–12 universe, and the quality distribution of the sector as a whole.

Chapter 8

Private Schooling and the Public System

THE DEVELOPMENT OF AMERICAN PRIVATE EDUCATION

American private education predates the Declaration of Independence.[1] Though it started with mostly faith-based schools, the sector grew and diversified to include, among other things, private tutors and elite secular private academies. Though many of these options had associated costs, there were also a number of "free" private schools.[2]

Over time, however, some came to believe the country's diversity required a unifying force for the young. Others expressed an egalitarian concern, that an educational system comprised primarily of schools with nontrivial costs would inequitably distribute opportunity. Others were interested in combating growing levels of poverty in America's cities.

The combination of these factors helped energize the development of the nation's earliest "common" schools in the first half of the nineteenth century. These public schools gained traction with the passage of compulsory school attendance laws and the growing consensus that education was invaluable, even essential, especially for disadvantaged boys and girls. But even as public schools became increasingly popular, private education continued to grow. It has been estimated that enrollment in public secondary schools remained below private school enrollment until the 1880s.[3]

The expansion of private education was attributable to a number of factors, including the inability of public systems to build schools quickly enough; for a time, in cities such as Chicago, New York, and Philadelphia public schools had to turn away students due to insufficient capacity.[4] The greatest factor, however, was immigration and the associated upsurge in

107

Catholic schooling. Approximately 17 million immigrants entered the United States in the second half of the nineteenth century, many from heavily Catholic European nations.[5] At the turn of the twentieth century, America was 17 percent Catholic, up from only one percent at the time of the founding.[6] Millions more immigrants arrived in the first half of the twentieth century.

Anti-immigrant bigotry and the teaching of Protestantism in public schools precipitated America's Catholic bishops' 1884 decision to require all Catholic parishes to establish schools and their instruction that all Catholic parents send their children to these new schools. A half century later, the massive "Baby Boom" accelerated the demand for all types of schools. The consequence of these factors was the astonishing growth of Catholic primary and secondary education. In the years before the Civil War, there were only two hundred Catholic schools, but by 1965 there were nearly 13,500 serving 5.6 million students.[7]

Though the Catholic Church provided the majority of America's private schools for generations, many other faith traditions ran substantial numbers of schools. Episcopalians, Calvinists, Jews, Lutherans, Presbyterians, and Quakers all had schools by the mid-1800s. By the turn of the twentieth century, more faith communities developed networks of schools, including the Christian Reformed Church, Seventh-day Adventists, and Greek Orthodox.[8]

America's cities were home to the lion's share of these schools. About 360,000 students attended New York City's Catholic schools in 1960, almost 40 percent of the city's public school enrollment.[9] Other major cities in the Northeast and Midwest, including Boston, Chicago, and Pittsburgh, had substantial Catholic school populations. Lutheran schools became prevalent in the upper Midwest. Jewish day schools proliferated, especially in New York City. When the National Center on Education Statistics (NCES) first reported the location and religiosity of private schools (1989–90), nearly 40 percent of private schools were designated as located in a "central city."[10]

This sector remains robust to this day. According to NCES, as of the 2007–8 school year, there were more than 28,000 private schools nationwide serving nearly 5 million students, roughly equivalent to the entire population of the state of Colorado.[11] The non-public sector contributes more than one in five American K–12 schools.[12]

Private schools continue to have a disproportionate presence in urban America. Nearly ten-thousand private schools are located in cities. These schools were serving more than 2.1 million students in 2007–8. Faith-based institutions continue to dominate the sector, contributing three-quarters of private schools (both nationally and in cities).[13] Catholic education still contributes the preponderance, but its share has dropped consistently for two generations.[14]

These national figures translate into meaningful collections of private schools in America's cities. The Baltimore area has 153 private schools serving nearly thirty-thousand students. Houston has 228 private schools serving more than forty-six-thousand students.[15] America's two largest cities, New York City and Los Angeles, have 850 and 950 private schools respectively.[16]

America's private schools have a long history, and they represent a substantial portion of the urban K–12 system. Excluding them from the reform discussion, at the very least, leaves a gaping hole.

SEPARATING THE SECTORS

America's private schools have followed an unusual historical path compared to their international peers, ending in an uncommon position. Whereas other Western nations have policies that integrate "public" and "private" schools into a broader system or don't draw such sharp distinctions between the sectors, America's private schools are kept at arm's length from those run by the government.

These other nations demonstrate that America's approach to schools not run by the government is not the only one, and they call into question whether it is the best one. Both points are underscored by two historical facts: First, America's public and private schools weren't always separated in the way they are today; and second, we arrived at this current state of play through a tortuous succession of events.

In America's earliest days, there was little to no distinction between public, private, and religious schools. As historians Thomas Hunt and James Carper noted, "During the colonial and early national periods of American history, which spanned approximately two hundred years, religion and education were inextricably intertwined."[17] In the 1640s, Massachusetts Puritans required that all sufficiently large towns establish schools and that children be instructed in reading, civil law, and Christian doctrines.[18] Later in the seventeenth century, other colonies, including New York, Pennsylvania, South Carolina, and Virginia, encouraged religious instruction.[19]

In some locations in early nineteenth century America virtually all schools were run by religious organizations. In New York City, a group of leading Quakers, eventually known as the "Free School Society," was incorporated by the state and received state funds to start a school for poor children who were not receiving an education via another religious society.[20] However, through an evolutionary process spanning a century, the sectors were separated. A fascinating series of practices, political decisions, and court cases pushed private and public K–12 education into the distinct spheres known today.

One of the first steps was distinguishing who could run public schools. In New York City religious societies were denied common school funds beginning in 1825. This, notes historian Diane Ravitch, was a seminal moment, as a public school in that city was henceforth understood "to be not only free and open to all, but was to be devoid of religious sectarianism."[21]

"Sectarianism" was the operative word, and it was not synonymous with "faith" or "religion." The term was meant to distinguish the religious beliefs and practices of America's newest citizens from those of the nation's established majority. Some believed that the spread of Catholicism, Lutheranism, and other faiths threatened the nation's cohesion. Since these groups often sought to develop schools to teach students their native languages and pass down traditions and beliefs, their schools were often cast as "divisive, undemocratic, and inimical to the public interest."[22]

So despite its history and contributions, increasingly the private school sector was viewed critically. Nebraska passed a law prohibiting private schools from teaching any language other than English prior to ninth grade. Hawaii passed legislation seeking to severely regulate schools teaching foreign languages.

U.S. Representative James G. Blaine introduced an amendment to the U.S. Constitution that would have forbidden any government funding of schools run by sectarian religious organizations. In 1876, it passed overwhelmingly in the U.S. House of Representatives but fell two votes shy of the necessary two-thirds majority in the U.S. Senate. Nevertheless, the idea caught fire at the state level. Within fifteen years, twenty-nine states had added "Blaine Amendments" to their constitutions.[23] Today more than two-thirds of state constitutions have provisions prohibiting the public funding of faith-based schools.[24]

Even more notable were the efforts to bring private schooling to an end. In the late 1800s, Illinois and Wisconsin passed similar laws requiring students to attend public schools. Soon Oregon did the same.[25] But in a series of cases, the U.S. Supreme Court preserved private schooling and helped lay one half of the foundation for our current system of wholly separate education sectors. In 1923 and 1927, the Court ruled unconstitutional attempts to severely restrict the content of private education.

States do have the right to closely monitor and regulate the education of children, the Court determined, but Nebraska's and Hawaii's laws interfered with the right of families to direct the upbringing of their children. In the latter case, the justices wrote that the law in question "would deprive parents of fair opportunity to procure for their children instruction which they think important…(the parent in question) has the right to direct the education of his own child without unreasonable restrictions." [26]

The Court reached a similar conclusion in the famous 1925 case of *Pierce v. Society of Sisters*. Ruling unconstitutional Oregon's law requiring children to attend public schools, the justices noted that the "inevitable practical result of enforcing the Act under consideration would be destruction" of the private schools directly involved in the case "and perhaps all other private primary schools for normal children within the State of Oregon." Such schools were involved in work "long regarded as useful and meritorious." The Court concluded famously, "The child is not the mere creature of the State." [27]

Through these 1920s decisions, it was settled that religious and other non-government organizations were permitted to operate K–12 schools and that parents had the right to choose them for their children.

RELIGION AND PUBLIC SCHOOLS

Interestingly, the antagonism to private education did *not* result from a national consensus that religion and education had to be separated. In fact, religion had been a part of public education for years and continued in that role for decades to come. Across the nation, countless public schools continued to teach "nondenominational" Protestantism. Such practices had a long pedigree. Horace Mann, the father of "common schools," supported the use of the Bible in public schools. [28]

In 1844 the New York City Board of Education ruled that a school's requiring its students to read the Bible did not constitute sectarianism. [29] A number of state courts during this era rendered similar decisions, for instance upholding the right of schools to use the Bible as a textbook and to require students to bow their heads during prayers. [30]

Faith and public education were tangled in other ways. In the early twentieth century, the "Gary Plan" (named after the Indiana city where it got its start), which excused public school students during the school day to attend religious classes, gained steam nationwide. Districts in forty-eight states sponsored such "release-time" programs by 1923. [31] Apart from the Bible, other textbooks were either explicitly or implicitly religious, including the ubiquitous *McGuffey Readers*, which sold well over 100 million copies. [32]

But over time, religion was slowly but comprehensively removed from public schools, providing the second half of the foundation for today's arrangements. Among the earliest activities was an 1890 decision of the Wisconsin's supreme court, which declared Bible reading in public schools illegal. But, according to scholar John Witte, the bulk of activity in this area occurred between 1947 and 1985 through a series of U.S. Supreme Court decisions.[33]

In the seminal 1947 case of *Everson v. Board of Education*, the Court wrote, "No tax in any amount, large or small, can be levied to support any religious activities or institutions, whatever they may be called, or whatever form they may adopt to teach or practice religion."[34] Constitutional scholar Douglas Laycock has described this as the "no-aid principle," a precedent that largely governed cases involving U.S. private schools for the next half century.[35]

In 1948, the Court struck down a state policy that allowed release-time religious activities to be held on public school grounds.[36] In 1962, the famous *Engel v. Vitale* decision held that a state-composed prayer for public school students, even if voluntary, was unconstitutional.[37] Soon thereafter, the Court decided that Bible-reading and the saying of the Lord's Prayer in public schools were unconstitutional.[38]

During this era the Court declared unconstitutional salary subsidies for private school teachers, tuition reimbursements, the provision of certain supplies to private schools, and more. In its 1971 *Lemon v. Kurtzman* decision, the Court developed a three-part test for determining if a law in the realm of church-state controversy was constitutional. This "Lemon Test" elevated and strengthened the wall between private schools and public support.

The upshot of these activities and decisions was the bifurcation of the K–12 system along the lines understood today: a judicially protected private school system permitted to teach faith but excluded from nearly all forms of public support and public accountability, and a public school system devoid of religion but fully supported by public funds.

So for the several generations preceding the advent of chartering, a short-hand way of describing the entire American K–12 landscape was "the privately financed, mostly religious nonpublic school sector and the government-run public school sector."

PRIVATE SCHOOLS AND PUBLIC POLICY

This distinction has caused most of our education policies to treat schools from these two sectors completely differently. Of greatest significance is funding. State and local funding, approximately 90 percent of K–12 budgets, is directed almost completely toward public schools. Federal funding is similarly cordoned off.

Under the federal Elementary and Secondary Education Act, which includes the multi-billion dollar Title I program, all funds (and all materials purchased by such funds) must be controlled and administered by public agencies, not private schools. Similarly, services supported by these dollars cannot be provided by private schools, and all such services and materials must be "secular, neutral, and nonideological."

Almost as importantly, the standards, assessments, and accountability provisions required by the federal law only apply to public schools. So the tools used to make transparent what students are taught, measure what they learned, evaluate the effectiveness of schools, and intervene in those struggling don't pertain to the entire nonpublic sector. Public and private schools are treated differently in many other areas, including teacher certification and special education. Even large-scale, citywide reform initiatives like Chicago's "Renaissance 2010" and Philadelphia's "Imagine 2014" are directed at only public schools.

Some public policies influence the private education sector. Private schools are typically subject to accreditation and must meet health, safety, and building codes. Private schools are also subject to civil rights legislation (including prohibitions on discrimination based on race, color, national origin, sex, disability, and age). But in general, and in most material ways, our laws, regulations, and practices give little indication that private schools are part of a larger K–12 system.

INTERNATIONAL COMPARISONS OF PRIVATE EDUCATION

This arrangement is unusual when compared to our international peers. As scholars Charles Glenn and Jan De Groof catalogue in their international survey of private education, most nations have done far more to integrate their government-run and private schools.[39] Like the United States, in many of these nations, education and religion were tightly linked from the start. But unlike the United States, these nations built comprehensive, sector-crossing systems.

Most have explicit protections for private schools in their constitutions (Belgium, the Netherlands, Denmark, Germany, Greece, Spain, Canada, South Africa, etc.) or in law (Luxembourg, Sweden, Scotland, Iceland, Australia, etc.). Moreover, nearly all of these countries have a tradition of funding their private schools.

In Spain, France, Ireland, and the Netherlands, non-government schools are guaranteed funding by the constitution. In Austria, Belgium, Italy, Finland, and others, the right to state financing is covered by other legal provisions. In a number of countries, like Canada, Germany, and South Africa, the courts have protected and shaped the rules allowing state aid to private schools. In a number of nations, private schools are guaranteed the same funding levels as government schools. In many of these nations, religious schools are treated the same as secular private schools.

In England and Wales, Catholic and Protestant schools are considered part of the public system. In 2009, the Australian government invested more than $400 million of new funding in Catholic and independent schools in exchange for greater financial transparency.[40] The United States is in limited company (Greece, Bulgaria, Scotland) with its overarching prohibition on aid to non-government schools.

Many of those nations permitting such aid have developed sensible methods for protecting private schools' right to be different while ensuring the public's right to accountability. In the Netherlands, private schools receive full funding but must follow the nation's core curriculum, though with freedom to achieve goals in distinctive ways. In Finland, once approved by the state, private schools may develop programs different from government schools.

Swedish private schools develop work plans explaining how national requirements will be met; Iceland and Norway follow a similar model. Australian private schools must follow the curriculum established by their respective states, but they may supplement this with material aligned with their religious mission or educational philosophy. In Austria, Ireland, Denmark, New Zealand and other nations, private schools have even greater autonomy.

In the United States, attempts to treat the two sectors more similarly have run into obstacles. Supreme Court decisions have struck down a number of private-school-friendly state programs. The political branches too have posed challenges. During the 1960s and 1970s several attempts were made in Congress to provide aid to private schools via means that may have passed constitutional muster. These efforts, however, failed to generate sufficient support on Capitol Hill and the other end of Pennsylvania Avenue. Likewise, numerous state-level attempts to pass school voucher programs have been turned back over the years.

All of these factors raise important abstract questions about our public policies related to private schools. But they have also had a very real practical consequence that compels us to ask whether our current system is sensible: the staggeringly rapid disappearance of inner-city faith-based schools.

Under current conditions, not only is the private schools sector unable to take advantage of the four systemic innovations outlined in chapter 7, one of those mechanisms—closures—has actually been distorted in a way that compromises instead of strengthens this sector.

In a rational system, a school's lifespan would be a function of its quality. But in the case of urban private schools, this link has been severed. A tidal wave of closures is swamping the sector, washing high- and low-performing schools alike out with the receding tide.

THE DISAPPEARANCE OF INNER-CITY PRIVATE SCHOOLS

To little public notice, in 1972 the White House issued a report on the perilous state of America's private schools. Crafted by the "President's Panel on Nonpublic Education," the report painted a dire picture of the sector's prospects. Schools were closing at a rate of one per day due to falling enrollments and climbing costs. The group issued a stern warning. "If decline continues, pluralism in education will cease, parental options will virtually terminate and public schools will have to absorb millions of American students."

They recognized that this problem was localized in cities and had tragic implications for the disadvantaged. At that time more than 80 percent of private schools were in urban communities, and in America's twenty largest cities, nearly 40 percent of students attended nonpublic schools. Continued closures would severely influence "large urban centers, with especially grievous consequences for poor and lower middle-class families in racially changing neighborhoods where the nearby nonpublic school is an indispensable stabilizing factor."[41]

The report also noted the challenges faced by faith-based schools. "The crisis is most acutely felt by church-related schools," they wrote, later adding that although Catholic schools were particularly hard hit, "the problem is not exclusively theirs." Other faiths' schools were suffering as well. Though the private character of these schools may have caused many to pay little heed, the report took a different approach. It included a section called "The Public Interest," which made the case that these schools contributed to the common good by providing diversity in schooling, choice to families, and competition to the public system.

Moreover, the schools' willingness to "enroll a significant number of children who are not adherents to their faith" demonstrated that they were about education and service, not merely proselytization. Indeed, the full report was titled, *Nonpublic Education and the Public Good.* The report ended on a solemn but stirring note: "The next few years are critical to the future of pluralism in education. Whatever is done must be undertaken with a profound sense of urgency."

Tragically, little was done, and the distressing trends continued for decades. Data from the National Catholic Educational Association indicates that Catholic schools began declining in 1965. Over the next forty-five years more than five thousand schools would be lost. Enrollment fell by more than 60 percent.[42] From 1966 to 2000, the Lutheran Church–Missouri Synod lost scores of schools, and enrollment fell by more than twenty-thousand students.[43]

Most of these losses were suffered in large urban areas, particularly in the Northeast and upper Midwest. From 1998 to 2009, the Catholic Archdiocese of Detroit lost sixty-five schools, Chicago lost sixty-four, and Newark, fifty-three. During this span, fourteen dioceses lost ten or more schools.[44] Federal data revealed that losses were hitting virtually the entire faith-based urban education sector. Between 1990 (the first year NCES collected such data) and 2006, central-city Lutheran schools saw a 13 percent decrease; central-city Baptist schools, 28 percent; and central-city Seventh-day Adventist schools, 39 percent.[45]

From 2000 to 2006, losses accelerated: 27 percent of central-city Episcopal schools closed, 38 percent of central-city Pentecostal schools closed, and 40 percent of central-city Assembly of God schools closed.[46] The Association of Christian Schools International reported the loss of more than 30 percent of its urban schools between 2000 and 2007.[47]

In 2008, the White House Domestic Policy Council released a comprehensive study on the status of inner-city religious schools. Titled *Preserving a Critical National Asset: America's Disadvantaged Students and the Crisis in Faith-based Urban Schools*, the report in many ways mirrored the White House publication of thirty-six years earlier. Among its most startling findings was that between 2000 and 2006, 1,200 faith-based urban schools had been lost, displacing 425,000 students. It noted the number of schools closed was "comparable to the size of the entire Los Angeles Unified School District, the second largest public school district in the Nation."[48] It concluded that tragically the losses were likely to accelerate not subside in the years to come.

These predictions were sadly confirmed as a number of dioceses planned new rounds of closures. Brooklyn announced its intentions to shutter more than a dozen schools.[49] The Archdiocese of Washington contemplated closing or reconfiguring as many as fourteen.[50] Philadelphia planned to close or consolidate nearly fifty schools.[51] One recent study, noting that a five-decade realignment process was catching up to these schools, suggested that the pace of losses might be accelerating.[52] A 2006 study reported that 80 percent of Catholic school leaders said that it had become "very much" more challenging to finance their schools over the previous five years.[53]

These closures are the consequence of an unsustainable financial model. Beginning in the mid-1900s, urban America underwent major changes. Many upwardly mobile working-class and more affluent city residents moved to the suburbs, and significant numbers of low-income African-Americans and Latinos replaced them in central cities. As a result, urban nonpublic schools' two main sources of income were compromised: students were less able to pay tuition, and smaller, poorer parishes couldn't subsidize their schools as before.

A 1990 report on Lutheran schools sounded an alarm, noting that this formula was making school endowments all but essential.[54] Similarly, in 2008, a national leader of Jewish day schools noted that private philanthropy was the only thing enabling its urban schools to stay afloat.[55] In 2005, inner-city Catholic schools relied on fundraising and subsidies of various sorts for nearly half of their income.[56]

At the same time, costs were growing. Shrinking numbers of low-cost nuns, priests, and brothers available to teach in Catholic schools forced dioceses to hire growing numbers of higher-cost lay teachers and administrators. The inherent expense of this shift was exacerbated by the necessity of competing for human capital with urban public school districts, which were consistently raising salaries.

The starting salary for a beginning New York City public school teacher is over $45,000; nationwide, the average salary of public elementary/middle school principals approximately $80,000.[57] But a 2006 study found that the average Catholic elementary school principal had an annual salary of $50,000, and a starting inner-city Catholic teacher earned less than $26,000.[58]

Urban nonpublic schools also faced significant capital costs. Many of their facilities were deteriorating, having been constructed at the turn of the previous century or earlier when immigration was at its peak. A 2007 survey found that the average Catholic school in operation was founded in 1933, with 25 percent founded before 1910.[59] The median year of newest construction for these schools is 1964 and certainly earlier for the poorest, inner-city schools.[60]

It is important to note that urban public schools toil in the same difficult conditions. They too must address the challenges of high poverty, and their expenses are also extensive. The difference is that urban public schools receive sizable, reliable streams of government aid. Nonpublic schools do not.

The disappearance of inner-city faith-based schools provides another compelling reason for including private education in the school reform discussion. Far from being enclaves of the privileged, most of these schools are educating disadvantaged students—the same students in traditional and charter public schools. When the urban exodus of white and middle-income families occurred, most of these schools committed to staying in their neighborhoods and serving the next generation of at-risk children. A 2006 study found that religious private schools serve less "elitist" populations than nonsectarian private schools.[61]

The schools' fundamental message remained unchanged; as one study described it, "It doesn't matter where you come from or how little money your family may have; we expect you to work hard, to behave, and in time to succeed."[62] This conviction was consistent irrespective of students' race, wealth, or faith.

Despite once serving virtually only Lutheran children, by the early 1980s more than 40 percent of Lutheran school students were members of other faith communities.[63] By 2008, 75 percent of students in Episcopal schools were non-Episcopalians; a number of these schools, as part of the "Episcopal Urban School Alliance," served predominantly inner-city, minority students.[64] Often Friends schools in urban communities educate almost entirely non-Quaker student bodies. In many of these schools, more than half of the students are low-income and/or racial minorities.[65]

Today, Catholic schools report serving well over three-hundred-thousand non-Catholic students, most of whom live in urban areas.[66] In 2005, more than five hundred Catholic schools had student bodies that were less than 25 percent Catholic.[67] In the Archdiocese of New York, more than 35,000 children attend its inner-city schools, 66 percent of whom live at or below the poverty line, and more than half of whom live in single-parent homes; 94 percent of these students are minority.[68]

In a particularly vulnerable set of inner-city Pittsburgh Catholic schools, nearly all of the students are minority, and 75 percent qualify for free or reduced-price lunch.[69] A Boston College survey of inner-city Catholic elementary schools found that three-quarters of their students were racial minorities.[70] In 2007, seven Catholic schools in Washington, D.C., were on the brink of closure; nearly all of their students were minority, 65 percent qualified for free or reduced-price lunch, and less than a third were Catholic.[71]

Because of these schools' dedication and demographics, one scholar wrote that they "are playing a liberating role for tens of thousands of underprivileged American children."[72] *The Wall Street Journal* described them as "an educational lifeline" for the poor.[73] In many of these impoverished neighborhoods, a nonpublic school serves as a powerful stabilizing force. Its loss could undermine vulnerable students and families. Private school closures in under-resourced communities reduce the already limited education options available. The popularity of publicly funded school choice programs and private scholarship offerings, evidenced by great demand and long waiting lists, attests to the great value inner-city parents assign to school alternatives.

Another reason to pay greater attention to this issue is purely financial. When inner-city faith-based schools close, their students generally return to public schools. This comes with a major price tag. One report estimated that the Catholic school closures over the last two decades have cost taxpayers more than $20 billion because public schools have had to unexpectedly absorb hundreds of thousands of students.[74]

But the final and potentially most important reason to be distressed by these closures is that good schools are vanishing. Closures are now the consequence of neighborhood poverty instead of academic failure. In the long term, this inhibits the development of a healthy system of schools. But in the short term, the effects are heartbreaking: a safe, successful urban private school working wonders for low-income children is highly susceptible to financial unsustainability and therefore closure. As the next chapter will discuss, this is far more than a hypothetical debate: The high quality of many of these schools is unquestionable.

When the full panoply of causes and consequences are considered, the isolation of private schools from the broader urban public school system can seem tragic and illogical. Urban private schools have a long history, and they continue to contribute a significant share of the K–12 landscape in inner cities. For years, they served many of the nation's most disadvantaged immigrant children, and today they serve huge numbers of low-income African-American and Latino boys and girls.

No matter how compelling their results or needy their students, urban private schools are denied direct access to nearly all streams of public funding, forcing families to pay tuition and schools to raise money privately. They seldom benefit from major public school initiatives. They don't partake in the standards and accountability movement. Closures are displacing countless students and generating costs for public schools. And serving as a backdrop for this entire scenario are the numerous Western nations that have devised sensible methods for supporting private schools without harming public schools.

TOWARD A SOLUTION

A touchstone of this book is that our most important goal should be enabling as many urban students as possible to access high-quality schools. The story of private schools reveals how our policies are inhibiting the realization of this goal. In thinking through possible solutions, our point of departure ought to be something along the lines of, "How can we enable this valuable but threatened sector of schools to more fully contribute to the education of urban students?" Or, better yet, "How can we best integrate private schools into a high-performing system of urban K–12 education?"

Unfortunately, though there are many private school advocates, little to no work has proceeded along these lines. Those committed to urban private education have typically pursued a set of strategies with one objective in mind: acquisition of government aid. This is necessary, but it is not sufficient. Funding alone won't help integrate private schools into a broader system or help that system become high-functioning. It won't guarantee new schools or high-quality human capital. Moreover, funding-only proposals in the form of vouchers and tax credit programs have frequently failed politically, and for those open to a broader discussion about private schools and the public system, a funding-only approach will seem incomplete.

Fortunately, the attempts to date to access government support have taught us much about the possibilities and pitfalls of the larger task of multi-sector integration. First, policies that enable urban private schools to access reliable streams of income can preserve at-risk schools. The *Milwaukee Journal-Sentinel* reported on how the city's voucher program helped the finances of a school on the brink. "St. Anthony School has a history stretching back decades, but it exists today only because of Milwaukee's voucher program."[75] Pennsylvania's tax credit program has been credited with shoring up Pittsburgh's previously struggling twelve Catholic high schools.[76]

Second, the political and judicial battles fought over these programs have been instructive. The most common political counter-argument is that they divert funding from public schools. But there are ways around this fight. The Pennsylvania tax credit program carves out funding for traditional public schools as well as private school scholarships. By making new dollars available to both sectors, the program has garnered such bipartisan support that it has been expanded several times.[77]

The federally funded Washington, D.C., scholarship program was able to win over many voucher opponents because it provided new funding in equal amounts for scholarships, charters, and traditional public schools.[78] This "three-sector" approach demonstrated that the funding of private schools could be part of a multi-sector strategy.

Another concern relates to accountability. Policymakers want to ensure that private schools receiving government funds are providing a rigorous education. The Milwaukee voucher program addresses quality concerns through the "New Schools Approval Board," a government-authorized body that controls which private schools participate. In its first year, the board denied sixteen of nineteen applications, thereby, in the words of the city's major newspaper, "beginning its life with a powerful statement that it will stop any school it doesn't think is prepared to provide a quality education from getting off the ground."[79]

The Washington, D.C., voucher legislation included a multi-year performance evaluation. An outside entity was charged with comparing the academic gains of participating students and a tightly matched control group. Louisiana's voucher initiative was written with several accountability provisions. Private schools must be deemed eligible by the state, and scholarship students attending private schools must take all assessments required by the state's accountability system.[80]

The biggest concern, however, has been the alleged discord with the First Amendment. But there is reason to believe these objections can be addressed. Beginning in 1986, the Court became increasingly open to allowing government programs to fund religious institutions, including schools. Since then the Court has upheld six such programs while invalidating none.[81]

Laycock argues that the loss of Catholic schools has actually helped the pro-funding cause. When Catholic schools comprised nearly 90 percent of the private education sector, public aid to nonpublic schools translated in many minds to the funding of a single religion. Now that the Catholic share has decreased (to approximately 40 percent of enrollment), making the sector more diverse, such funding is more easily seen as a means of "achieving neutrality across a wide range of views."

The Supreme Court's seminal case *Zelman v. Simmons-Harris* (2002) determined how a funding program could pass constitutional muster. The Court upheld an Ohio voucher program because aid was directed to families: the government supported parental choice not religious schools. So long as state aid reaches a private school indirectly, the program doesn't constitute unlawful government support of religion. So states can use properly written scholarship tax credit and voucher programs to bring private schools into the fold.

CONCLUSION

A series of events over 150 years distanced urban private schools from their public peers. But more recent events have suggested a way to bridge the gap and begin constructing a comprehensive system of schools. Public money can reach private schools without offending the Constitution. These programs can help students access better options and preserve financially struggling schools. Political animus can be reduced by developing a funding mechanism fair to all schools involved. Participating private schools can be subject to public accountability.

These principles guide the recommendations—found in the book's final section—related to private schools and show how some or all private schools can be fairly integrated into a new public school system. But this system would more than merely level the playing field; it would enable us to apply the systemic innovations of chartering across this entire K–12 landscape. We'd be positioned to encourage a diverse array of new starts across the entire system, evaluate all schools based on their quality, and then apply interventions to schools based on their quality and irrespective of sector.

But before getting there, one last issue must be addressed. Does the distribution of quality within the urban private schools sector make it amenable to the systemic innovations of chartering?

NOTES

1. Domestic Policy Council, *Preserving a Critical National Asset: America's Disadvantaged Students and the Crisis in Faith-Based Urban Schools* (Washington, DC: The White House, September 2008).

2. See Diane Ravitch. *The Great School Wars: A History of the New York City Public Schools* (Baltimore, MD: Johns Hopkins University Press, 2000).

3. David Tyack, *The One Best System*, 56.

4. Tyack, *The One Best System*, 71.

5. Frederick C. Croxton, *Statistical Review of Immigration, 1820–1910*, Report of the Immigration Commission to the Senate Committee on Immigration (Washington, DC: Government Printing Office, 1911).

6. Tyack, *The One Best System*, 86.

7. Dale McDonald and Margaret Schultz, *United States Catholic Elementary and Secondary Schools 2008–2009: The Annual Statistical Report on Schools, Enrollment and Staffing* (Arlington, VA: National Catholic Educational Association, 2009).

8. James Carper and Thomas Hunt, "Religion and Education in the United States: An Introduction," in *The Praeger Handbook of Religion and Education in the United States*, vol. 1, eds. James C. Carper and Thomas Hunt (Westport, CT: Praeger Publishing, 2009), 8–9, 17–18, 22.

9. See Appendix in Ravitch, *The Great School Wars.*

10. Elizabeth Gerald, Marilyn McMillen, and Steven Kaufmann, *Private School Universe Survey, 1989–90*, (Washington, DC: National Center for Education Statistics, Institute of Education Sciences, U.S. Department of Education, 1992), http://nces.ed.gov/pubs93/93122.pdf.

11. Stephen Broughman, et al., *2007–08 Private School Universe Survey (PSS) Data File User's Manual and Survey Documentation* (Washington, DC: National Center for Education Statistics, Institute of Education Sciences, U.S. Department of Education, 2009); and Table 5 in Thomas D. Snyder, Sally A. Dillow, and Charlene M. Hoffman, *Digest of Education Statistics 2008* (Washington, DC: National Center for Education Statistics, Institute for Education Sciences, U.S. Department of Education, 2009).

12. See Table 87, in Snyder, Dillow, and Hoffman, *Digest of Education Statistics 2008.*

13. Broughman, et al., *2007–08 Private School Universe Survey.*

14. In 1965, nearly 90 percent of private school students attended Catholic schools; today, it is approximately 40 percent.

15. Data generated through "Search for Private Schools," *Private School Universe Survey*, National Center for Education Statistics, Institute for Education Sciences, U.S. Department of Education, http://nces.ed.gov/surveys/pss/privateschoolsearch/.

16. Broughman, et al., *2007–08 Private School Universe Survey.*

17. Carper and Hunt, "Religion and Education in the United States."

18. Ravitch, *The Great School Wars*, 7; Carper and Hunt, "Religion and Education in the United States."

19. Lawrence A. Cremin, *American Education: The Colonial Experience 1607–1783* (New York: Harper & Row, 1970).

20. Ravitch, *The Great School Wars*, 9–11.

21. Ravitch, *The Great School Wars*, 21.

22. Charles Leslie Glenn, *The Myth of the Common School* (Amherst: University of Massachusetts Press, 1988), quoted in Carper and Hunt, "Religion and Education in the United States."

23. Joseph Viteritti, "Framing the Issue: Liberty, Equality, and Opportunity in Historical Perspective," in *Proceedings of the White House Summit on Inner-city Children and Faith-based Schools* (Washington, DC: The White House, April 24, 2008).

24. Anthony Picarello, "Constitutional Parameters on Government Assistance to Faith-based Urban Schools," in *Proceedings of the White House Summit on Inner-city Children and Faith-based Schools*.

25. Carper and Hunt, "Religion and Education in the United States."

26. *Meyer v. State of Nebraska*, 262 U.S. 390 (1923) and Farrington v. Tokushige, 273 U.S. 284 (1927).

27. *Pierce v. Society of Sisters*, 268 U.S. 510 (1925).

28. Carper and Hunt, "Religion and Education in the United States," 6–8.

29. Ravitch, *The Great School Wars*, 80.

30. See *Donahoe v. Richards*, 38 Me. 376 (1854) and *Spiller v. Inhabitants of Woburn*, 12 Allen 127 (Mass. 1866).

31. Ronald D. Cohen and Raymond A. Mohl, *The Paradox of Progressive Education: The Gary Plan and Urban Schooling* (Port Washington, NY: Kennikat Press, 1979).

32. Carper and Hunt, "Religion and Education in the United States."

33. John Witte, Jr., *Religion and the American Constitutional Experiment*, Second Edition. (Boulder, CO: Westview Press, 2005).

34. *The Oyez Project, Everson v. Board of Education*, 330 U.S. 1 (1947).

35. Douglas Laycock, "Why the Supreme Court Changed Its Mind About Government Aid to Religious Institutions: It's a Lot More than Just Republican Appointments," *Brigham Young University Law Review* 2 (March 1, 2008): 275–294.

36. *McCollum v. Board of Education Dist. 71* , 333 U.S. 203 (1948).

37. *Engel v . Vitale* , 370 U.S. 421 (1962).

38. *Abington School District v. Schempp* , 374 U.S. 203 (1963).

39. Charles L. Glenn and Jan De Groof, *Balancing Freedom, Autonomy and Accountability in Education*, vol. 1 (The Netherlands: Wolf Legal Publishers, 2005), 267–310.

40. Miki Perkins, "State hands $2.1bn to non-government schools," *The Age*, November 12, 2009.

41. The President's Panel on Nonpublic Education, *Nonpublic Education and the Public Good: Final Report* (Washington, DC: The White House, 1972).

42. McDonald and Schultz, *United States Catholic Elementary and Secondary Schools 2008–2009*.

43. Carper and Hunt, "Religion and Education in the United States," 32–33.

44. McDonald and Schultz, *United States Catholic Elementary and Secondary Schools 2008–2009*.

45. See Domestic Policy Council, *Preserving a Critical National Asset*.

46. Stephen P. Broughman and Lenore A. Colaciello, *Private School Universe Survey, 1999–2000* (Washington DC: U.S. Department of Education, Institute of Education Sciences, National Center for Education Statistics, 2001); and Stephen P. Broughman, Nancy L. Swaim, and Patrick W. Keaton, *Characteristics of Private Schools in the United States: Results From the 2005–2006 Private School Universe Survey* (Washington, DC: National Center for Education Statistics, Institute of Education Sciences, U.S. Department of Education, 2008).

47. Vernard Gant, "The Economic Plight of ACSI Urban Christian Schools," in *Proceedings of the White House Summit on Inner-city Children and Faith-based Schools*.

48. Domestic Policy Council, *Preserving a Critical National Asset*, 10.

49. Paul Vitello and Winnie Hu, "Brooklyn Diocese Moves to Shut 14 Schools," *The New York Times*, January 13, 2009.

50. Michael Birnbaum, "Archdiocese questions future of 14 D.C., Md. schools," *Washington Post*, November 24, 2009.

51. Martha Woodall, Susan Snyder, and Kristen A. Graham, "'Everyone Just Cried': 4 Catholic Schools to Close," *The Philadelphia Inquirer*, January 6, 2012.

52. Mark M. Gray and Mary L. Gautier, *Primary Trends, Challenges and Outlook: A Report on Catholic Elementary Schools* (Arlington, VA: National Catholic Educational Association, January 2006).

53. Gray and Gautier, *Primary Trends, Challenges and Outlook*, 136.

54. Edward Keuer, *The Lutheran Teacher: Ministry in Transition*, Monograph Series (River Forest, IL: Lutheran Education Association, Winter 1990).

55. David Zwiebel, "Philanthropy and Jewish Day Schools," in *Proceedings of the White House Summit on Inner-city Children and Faith-based Schools*.

56. Gray and Gautier, *Primary Trends, Challenges and Outlook*, 84.

57. Salary Schedule Effective May 19, 2008, "Certified Teachers Schedule," New York City Department of Education, http://schools.nyc.gov/nr/rdonlyres/eddb658c-be7f-4314-85c0-03f5a00b8a0b/0/salary.pdf; and Robert Bimonte, *Financing the Mission* (Arlington, VA: National Catholic Educational Association, 2006), 17.

58. Bimonte, *Financing the Mission*.

59. Mary Gautier and Mary Benyna, *Dollars & Sense 2006–2007: A Report for the National Catholic Educational Association Secondary Schools Department* (Washington, DC: Center for Applied Research in the Apostolate, Georgetown University), 18.

60. Gray and Gautier, *Primary Trends, Challenges and Outlook*, 71.

61. Danny Cohen-Zada and William Sander, *Private School Choice: The Effects of Religion and Religiosity* (Beer Sheva, Israel: Monaster Center for Economic Research, Ben-Gurion University of the Negev, February 2006).

62. Scott Hamilton, "Introduction," in *Who Will Save America's Urban Catholic Schools?*, ed. Scott Hamilton (Washington, DC: Thomas B. Fordham Institute, April 2008), 12–20.

63. Jon Diefenthaler, "Lutheran Schools in Transition," in *Religious Schools in the United States, K–12*, eds. Thomas C. Hunt and James C. Carper (New York: Garland, 1993), 420–423.

64. Daniel Heischman, "The Episcopal School Urban Alliance," in *Proceedings of the White House Summit on Inner-city Children and Faith-based Schools*.

65. Irene McHenry, "Urban Friends Education: Challenging the Mind, Nourishing the Spirit," in *Proceedings of the White House Summit on Inner-city Children and Faith-based Schools.*

66. McDonald and Schultz, *United States Catholic Elementary and Secondary Schools 2008–2009*, 22.

67. Gray and Gautier, *Primary Trends, Challenges and Outlook*, 75.

68. "Inner City Success," About Us, Superintendent of Schools, Archdiocese of New York, http://www.adnyeducation.org/about-us/inner-city-student-success/.

69. Ambrose Murray, "Going the Extra Mile in Pittsburgh," in *Proceedings of the White House Summit on Inner-city Children and Faith-based Schools*.

70. Joseph O'Keefe, "How to Save Catholic Schools: Let the Revitalization Begin," *Commonweal* 5, no. 6, March 25, 2005.

71. Andy Smarick, *Catholic Schools Become Charter Schools: Lessons from the Washington Experience* (Washington, DC: Seton Education Partners, September 2009), http://www.setonpartners.org/Seton_DC_Case_Study_FINAL.pdf.

72. Andrew Coulson, "Catholic Schools and the Common Good," Mackinac Center for Public Policy, April 28, 2005), http://www.mackinac.org/7069.

73. Mary Anastasia O'Grady, "Archbishop Timothy Dolan: Proudly Pro-Choice on Education," *Wall Street Journal*, May 11, 2009.

74. Hamilton, "Introduction."

75. Alan Borsuk, "Changes at St. Anthony Make It a School to Watch," *Milwaukee-Wisconsin Journal Sentinel*, March 9, 2008.

76. Ronald Bowes, "Corporate Tax Credits: Transforming Education in Pennsylvania," in *Proceedings of the White House Summit on Inner-city Children and Faith-based Schools*.

77. Bowes, "Corporate Tax Credits."

78. Anthony Williams, "The 'Three Sector' Approach in Washington, DC," in *Proceedings of the White House Summit on Inner-city Children and Faith-based Schools*.

79. Alan Borsuk, "Just 3 New Voucher Schools Approved," *Milwaukee-Wisconsin Journal Sentinel*, July 20, 2009.

80. See *Student Scholarships for Educational Excellence Program*, Louisiana Department of Education, http://doe.louisiana.gov/topics/scholarships_for_excellence.html ; Student Scholarships for Educational Excellence Program, Act 509, Louisiana House Bill 1347, 2008.

81. Laycock, "Why the Supreme Court Changed Its Mind About Government Aid to Religious Institutions."

Chapter 9

The Private Quality Curve

The twisting evolution of the private school sector has influenced the research on private school quality in noteworthy ways. First, since nonpublic schools have largely been defined as different and separate from public schools, most studies on private school performance have compared their results to those of public schools. In this way, the research is similar to charter performance research: The sector is considered a monolith, so the basic question has been, "Are these schools better or worse than traditional public schools?" Second, since Catholic schools have long made up the majority of urban private schools, significant research has focused on them.

But this book is interested in something different. The overriding concern here is maximizing the number of urban students in excellent schools and building a system that continuously grows the supply of great schools. So it matters little which sector is, on average, better than another.

Chapters 3 and 6 demonstrated that "average performance" is largely meaningless because of the enormous variation in quality among the lowest income urban schools within the traditional public sector and the charter sector.

Is the same thing true in the private school sector?

For decades, many have studied the performance of America's private schools. The federal government's National Assessment of Education Progress (NAEP) provides one measure and typifies the common approach. In presenting its top-line results, NAEP separates America's schools into two types (private and public schools) and then compares the scores. In further analyses, it shows the results for Catholic schools. NAEP typically finds that private (and Catholic) schools have higher scores. The 2009 math report, for example, notes dryly, "private school students outperform public school students."

In the last generation or so, a number of high-profile studies found a "private schools advantage." In research published in the 1980s, sociologist James Coleman and his colleagues found that private school students, particularly those in Catholic schools, had higher achievement levels than their public school peers even after controlling for important background characteristics.[1]

The prominent 1990 book *Politics, Markets, and America's Schools* found a similar advantage in the private sector.[2] In 1993, Anthony Bryk and colleagues' *Catholic Schools and the Common Good* also found higher achievement levels in Catholic schools, with especially pronounced positive effects for disadvantaged students.[3] More recently, other researchers have found similar results.[4] Derek Neal found that the Catholic sector had higher high school graduation rates, college-going rates, and college graduation rates.[5]

Paul Peterson and Elena Llaudet reported students in both secular and faith-based private schools have higher achievement scores than similar students in public schools.[6] Andrew Greeley found that Catholic schools have a positive academic influence on disadvantaged students.[7] And in a meta-analysis of the findings of many empirical studies, William Jeynes found a significant achievement advantage in religious private schools, again, with particularly strong benefits for underserved students.[8]

A significant number of studies on voucher programs have shown that participating students, particularly minority students, often benefit compared to similar students remaining in their assigned public schools, indirectly suggesting a private schools advantage.[9]

But the literature is not conclusive. One 2007 study found that when proper controls are applied, disadvantaged students attending urban public high schools fared as well as students attending private high schools.[10] Similarly, Dan Goldhaber found in 1996 that private schools didn't outperform public schools.[11] In a 2006 analysis of NAEP math data, Christopher Lubienski and Sarah Theule Lubienski reported that when important student characteristics are controlled, "the presumably advantageous 'private school effect' disappears, and even reverses in most cases."[12]

Other studies have found mixed results among different types of private schools.[13] And not all voucher research supports the contention that private schools, on the whole, generate higher student achievement.[14]

Despite their different approaches and occasionally disparate findings, all of these studies—and many more—share an important feature. Each seeks to generalize the achievement results of the private schools sector or of large swaths of the sector, like Catholic schools. The inclination to treat such schools as indistinguishable from one another may be understandable: They are part of a distinct category ("private"), many are part of a distinct sub-category ("Catholic," "Jewish day," "nonsectarian"), and many share common features (school uniforms, crosses on walls, etc.).

But the truth is more complicated and interesting. Just like the adjective "charter," "private" tells us little about the most meaningful characteristics of a school falling under this broad heading. The list of sub-categories is extensive, and the variety of schools in each is expansive. An elite secular suburban boarding school may have next to nothing in common with a tiny rural Baptist school or an inner-city Lutheran school. Even two diocesan Catholic schools could have vastly different staffing models, curricula, and student bodies.

Accordingly, we shouldn't expect "private" to tell us much about the quality of any one of these nearly thirty-thousand schools. There are the standouts, like Harlem's Rice High, which, for more than three decades, has "rescued at-risk African-American boys and turned them into responsible men who go on to college and then give back to the community."[15] Other similarly esteemed schools serving similar students include the Denver Street School, Memphis's Jubilee Schools, and the network of Cristo Rey High Schools. Forty-nine private schools won "blue ribbons" from the U.S. Department of Education in 2011, including a number in urban areas.[16]

But there is another end of the spectrum. There are private schools that fail to properly educate their students, lose accreditation, or worse. The *Milwaukee Journal Sentinel* estimated in 2005 that ten percent of private schools participating in that city's voucher program had "alarming deficiencies."[17] Based on our experience with other fields, we should expect many private schools to fall between these two extremes. In a 2009 Commentary in *Education Week* titled "Not All Private Schools Are Created Equal," scholar Bruce Baker speculated that evaluations of voucher programs haven't reported stronger results precisely because of the wide variation in urban private school quality.[18]

These anecdotes begin to suggest that urban private school quality is considerably varied. Given the results of the two other major K–12 sectors, we might wonder if the private school distribution looks the same.

THE QUALITY DISTRIBUTION OF URBAN PRIVATE SCHOOLS

Determining the quality distribution of a city's nonpublic schools poses enormous challenges. With a city's traditional public schools and charter public schools, the task is more straightforward. Since they administer the same state assessments in the same grades and use the same definitions for poverty and proficiency, comparing the schools within each sector was uncomplicated.

For the most part, private schools are not required by law to administer standardized assessments, and very few use the same state tests as the nearby public schools. While many private schools do use tests, consistency becomes the impediment. In any given city, some private schools may not administer any standardized assessment, and those that do may use different tests and may administer them in different grades. Even if a critical mass of a city's private schools had consistent data, accessing it is a challenge. Unlike public schools, private schools are generally not required by law to make these results public.

There are, however, instances where a sufficient number of factors fall into place to allow tentative conclusions to be drawn. Decade-old data from New York City is one example. After the New York State Education Department introduced new English language arts and math assessments in 1999, all schools in the Catholic Diocese of Brooklyn and the Archdiocese of New York participated in grades four and eight. A 2001 study on New York City used these data to compare Catholic schools to public schools, and in doing so revealed the quality distribution of interest here.[19]

The study reported each of the city's Catholic school's performance (mean scale score) on the assessments. Using the data on the English language arts test reported in the study, histograms were constructed to show the relative share of schools falling into each performance band (Figure 9.1).

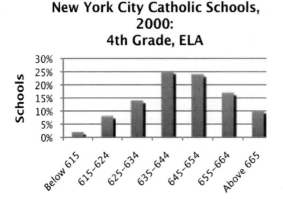

Figure 9.1a

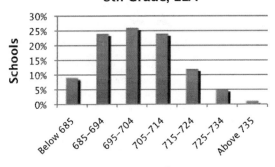

New York City Catholic Schools, 2000: 8th Grade, ELA

Figure 9.1b
Source: Charts based on data presented in *Catholic Schools in New York City*.

As was the case with the traditional and charter public school sectors in numerous urban areas, the performance of New York City's Catholic schools is widely distributed and bell-shaped. Schools' math scores follow the same pattern. But an important caveat is in order. These graphs represent all of the schools operated by the two dioceses that are located in the city, not just the lowest income schools, as was the case with the histograms in chapters 3 and 6 (where only schools with 60 percent FRPL and above were included).

While most of these schools serve large numbers of poor students, some have more affluent student bodies. So it could be the case that this distribution merely reflects the schools' varying levels of poverty. That is, it is possible that very poor schools have uniformly low scores and affluent schools have uniformly high scores. However, one of this study's major findings (paralleling previous findings by Coleman, Bryk, and others) is that the difference in performance among Catholic schools of different income levels is quite small, especially when compared to the varying performance levels of public schools of different means.[20]

The study reported that among a group of less poor Catholic schools (with an average student poverty rate of only 32 percent), seven percent of eighth graders scored in the lowest category in English language arts. Among a far lower income group of Catholic schools (each school averaging 90 percent student poverty), only a slightly higher percentage of students (nine percent) scored as poorly. Though it can't be said for certain based on the data available in the study, there is reason to suspect that a bell-shaped distribution would be seen among the subset of low-income Catholic schools as well.

While this report only captured Catholic school performance and not the entirety of the private school sector, its results are important. It exposes the considerable variability in achievement results among a large group of private schools in a single city (more than 250 schools). Given that a number of studies have found Catholic schools to be comparable to or better than other private schools, we might conclude that the distribution of the entire private sector looks similar (broad and bell-shaped) but possibly shifted slightly to the left.

PRIVATE SCHOOLS IN MILWAUKEE

Supporting evidence for this tentative conclusion is provided by a more recent study, one that provides possibly the best evidence available on the quality distribution of a city's entire private schools sector. In 2005, a new law governing Milwaukee's voucher program required that all participating private schools administer standardized assessments to their scholarship students in fourth, eighth, and tenth grades. Many chose nationally normed tests while others administered Wisconsin's state assessment. Researchers at the School Choice Demonstration Project standardized the results of each exam (converted scores to national percentiles) so the results from the various tests could be compared.

Although the purpose of the law was to enable comparisons between participating private schools and the traditional public school system, the data also facilitates our objective here: the comparison of schools *within* a city's private school sector (Figure 9.2). Also, since all of the school scores comprising the graphs below are composed from solely voucher recipients, the scores reflect a comprehensively low-income population.

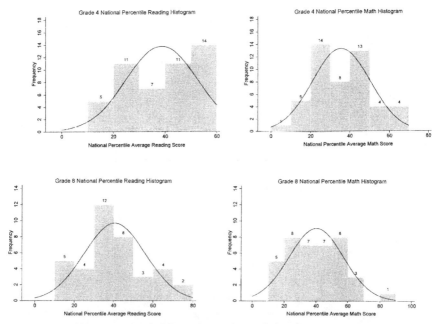

Figure 9.2 Performance of Milwaukee Private Schools
Source: Graphs appeared in the *Milwaukee Longitudinal School Choice Evaluation.*

Once again, the results for fourth and eighth grade reading and math reveal the same widely distributed, bell-shaped pattern.[21] The overarching point is worth reiterating. Entirely too often, observers would merely note that the average private school score was at about the 40th percentile nationally. Moreover, researchers would compare this average to the average score of public schools. But that analysis misses the more important point: Few of the private schools are actually *at* the 40th percentile. A sizeable number are below the 30th percentile or above the 50th, particularly at the eighth grade level.

Indeed, the authors of this report note the "positive skew" of the histograms, a small group of unusually high performers. This matches an important finding about the charter school quality distribution identified in chapter 6, where a number of cities had a disproportionate number of very-high-performing charters.

When the report's authors compared the private school distribution to the public school distribution, they found that the two looked remarkably similar. But there was one relevant exception: While the sectors had virtually identical shapes, the private sector had more variation in performance (a larger standard deviation). This they attributed to the greater diversity among participating private schools.

So, it looks like the normal process of comparing sectors based on the average performance of their schools has at least three critical flaws. First, it implies that we ought to be looking for one sector to be better than another. Second, it ignores the vast variation within each sector—a distribution that is similar from sector to sector. And third, it is unable to tell us anything about the difference in variation between sectors (in this case, private schools having more high performers and more low performers), which may be meaningful.

ADDITIONAL EVIDENCE

Though the two examples cited above point to the same conclusions, this might be insufficient evidence to substantiate the important claims at the heart of this study.

Though it is difficult to access the types of private school information needed here, an additional effort was made to confirm these results. For this book, school poverty rates and student test scores were requested from two large urban Catholic dioceses. The data were provided in exchange for a commitment of anonymity: the dioceses cannot be identified. Gaining access to these data sets has three important benefits. First, it provides consistent data across a significant number of private schools. In each diocese, the same assessment was used, and the same central office collected and reported performance and poverty levels.

Second, because the dioceses administer reading and math tests and collect free and reduced-price lunch levels, it allows for the same types of analyses conducted in chapters 3 and 6. Third, since these dioceses are so large, they encompass many schools, thereby increasing the likelihood of school variation and mirroring the sample size of a mid- to large-size urban public school district.

The results from these locations strongly corroborate the earlier findings. The first diocese provided math scores for fourth and eighth grades along with school poverty levels.[22] The schools in the diocese take the state's public school assessment (all of the diocese's schools are located within one state) and define "passing" or "proficiency" in the same way.

Though the diocese includes urban, rural, and suburban areas, in the graphs below only the schools in the diocese's major city are included. This was done to imitate as closely as possible the analyses in chapters 3 and 6; most urban public school districts encompass only or a vast majority of urban schools. The diocese's portfolio exhibits the same unmistakable pattern. In fourth grade, schools with the lowest levels of poverty have uniformly high proficiency rates. But as poverty levels increase, the variation among schools with similarly-resourced student bodies expands.

Among the schools with an FRPL level of 30 percent or less, the lowest passing rate is 86 percent (the highest is 100 percent). But among the schools with 100 percent poverty, passing rates range from 57 percent to 100 percent. In eighth grade, the clear heteroskedasticity seen earlier reappears, with poverty decreasing as a reliable predictor of achievement as poverty rates climb (Figure 9.3). As seen in chapter 3, school performance falls not along a line, but within a right triangle. Schools with less than 20 percent poverty have proficiency scores ranging from 73 percent to 100 percent. The range for schools with poverty levels around 30 percent extends from 47 percent to 100 percent.

The lowest-performing school at 60 percent poverty has 40 percent proficiency while the highest has 100 percent. And schools with the very highest levels of poverty show the greatest variation. In fact, two schools with virtually identical FRPL rates (95 percent and 96 percent, respectively) have radically dissimilar passing rates (12 percent and 100 percent).

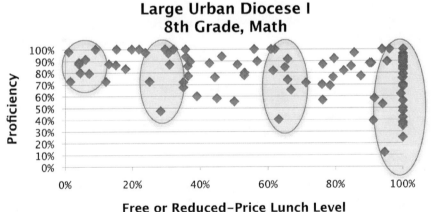

**Large Urban Diocese I
8th Grade, Math**

Figure 9.3

As in previous chapters, histograms have been created to show the distribution in quality among just the lowest income schools, those with at least three of five students qualifying for free or reduced-price lunch. Figure 9.4 shows the wide variability among school performance in fourth grade. Just as in the Milwaukee examples above and the traditional public and charter public examples in earlier chapters, by eighth grade the familiar bell-shaped distribution because more apparent.

Though the 80 percent to 89 percent decile has the largest contingent of observations, schools fall across the entire distribution. As was the case with other sectors, knowing that a certain urban school run by this diocese serves a high percentage of low-income students gives you almost no sense of how well its students are performing.

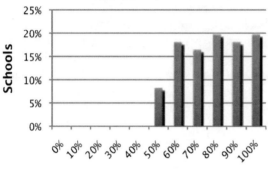

Figure 9.4a

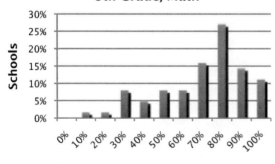

Figure 9.4b

The second urban diocese administers a "nationally normed" assessment, a test that compares a school's results to other schools across the country.[23] So a school's performance level—say, 60 percent—indicates that the school has a higher average performance level (in the grade and subject specified) than 60 percent of the nation's schools.

This diocese provided testing information for its schools in grades 3, 5, and 7, as well as each school's free or reduced-price lunch level. The results reveal the same patterns. School performance remains negatively correlated with income, but there is significant performance variation among the diocese's poorest schools (Figure 9.5). Also, as seen previously, this variation is larger in higher grades than in lower: in this diocese, though in each grade the variance among the schools with at least 80 percent FRPL rates is higher than among schools with 20 percent or less, the difference is considerably larger in fifth and seventh grades.[24]

Large Urban Diocese II
7th Grade, Math

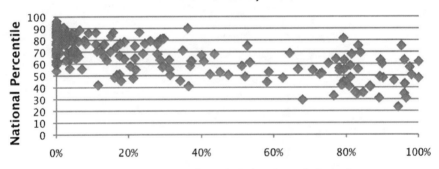

Figure 9.5

When turned into histograms using only the lowest-income schools, the same broad pattern emerges (Figure 9.6). In math, in all three grades, the largest group of schools is between the 40th and 50th percentile nationally. But there are numerous schools far above and below this median. In third grade, the average school is at the 43rd percentile, but one school is at the 93rd and another is at the 16th. In fifth grade, the average school is at the 45th percentile, while one is at the 85th and another is at the 16th.

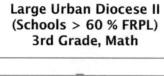

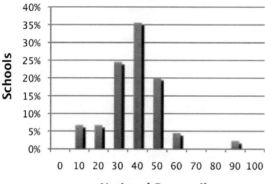

Figure 9.6a

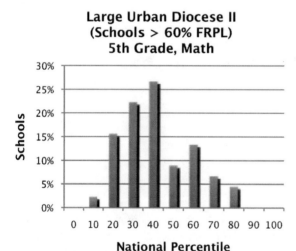

Figure 9.6b

The same pattern holds in reading (Figure 9.7). At each grade, there is wide variation in the quality of schools at the lowest income levels. In third grade, though the average school is at the 41st percentile, the highest and lowest are separated by nearly 70 national percentile points. In seventh grade, the highest and lowest schools are more than 20 percentile points from the diocese average.

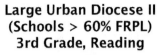

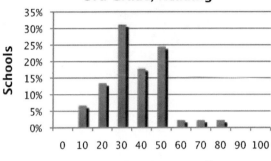

Figure 9.7a

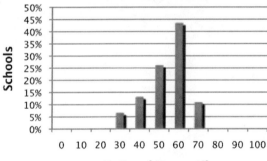

Figure 9.7b

CONCLUSION

Despite the years of wrangling over the performance of private schools vis-à-vis traditional public schools, the examples discussed in this chapter provide more reason to believe that such an approach is misguided. There is wide variation in the quality of private schools in urban America, even among the narrower subset of very low-income schools. This is the same conclusion reached with regard to the other urban school sectors. Knowing to which sector an urban school belongs—even if you know the average achievement of that sector—reveals very little about its performance.

Though these facts are important, if policy-making is your lens, switching perspective from the school level to school cohorts (cohorts defined by quality) reveals an even more valuable conclusion. Should you study a city's most academically troubled schools you'd find traditional public, charter public, and private schools. Should you study its best schools, you'd find the same mix.

So if we want more great schools and fewer failing ones, and, for the sake of practicality, we know our starting point must be the universe of schools we currently have, what should we do? That is the subject of the final section of this book.

NOTES

1. For example, see James S. Coleman, Thomas Hoffer, and Sally Kilgore, *High School Achievement: Public, Catholic, and Private Schools Compared* (New York: Basic Books, 1982) and James S. Coleman and Thomas Hoffer, *Public and Private High Schools: The Impact of Communities* (New York: Basic Books, 1987).

2. John E. Chubb and Terry M. Moe, *Politics, Markets and America's Schools* (Washington, DC: Brookings Institution Press, 1990).

3. Anthony S. Bryk, Peter B. Holland, and Valerie E. Lee, *Catholic Schools and the Common Good* (Cambridge, MA: Harvard University Press, 1993).

4. See also Raymond Domanico, *Catholic Schools in New York City* (New York: New York University, Program on Education and Civil Society, March 2001); Adam Gamoran, "Student Achievement in Public Magnet, Public Comprehensive, and Private City High Schools," *Educational Evaluation and Policy Analysis* 18, no. 1 (January 1, 1996): 1–18; Leslie A. Scott, et al., "Two Years Later: Cognitive Gains and School Transitions of NELS:88 Eighth Graders" (Washington, DC: National Center for Education Statistics, Office of Educational Research and Improvement, U.S. Department of Education, 1995); and Derek Neal and Jeffrey Grogger, "Further Evidence on the Effects of Catholic Secondary Schooling," *Brookings-Wharton Papers on Urban Affairs: 2000* (Washington, DC: Brookings Institution Press), 151–93.

5. Derek Neal, "The Effects of Catholic Secondary Schooling on Educational Achievement," *Journal of Labor Economics* 15, no. 1 (January 1997): 98–123.

6. Paul E. Peterson and Elena Llaudet, "On the Public-Private School Achievement Debate" (paper presented at annual meeting of the American Political Science Association, Philadelphia, PA, August 2006).

7. Andrew Greeley, *Catholic High Schools and Minority Students* (New Brunswick, NJ: Transaction Publishers, 2002).

8. See William H. Jeynes, "Religion, Intact Families, and the Achievement Gap," *Interdisciplinary Journal of Research on Religion* 3 (2007), Article 3; and William H. Jeynes, "The Academic Contributions of Faith-based Schools," in *Proceedings of the White House Summit on Inner-city Children and Faith-based Schools*.

9. For example, see William G. Howell, et al., *The Education Gap: Vouchers and Urban Schools* (Washington, DC: Brookings Institution Press, 2006) and "Appendix Table 2: The Effect of School Choice on Families that Exercise Choice," in Jay Greene, *A Survey of Results from Voucher Experiments: Where We Are and What We Know*, Civic Report (New York: Manhattan Institute for Policy Research, July 2000).

10. Harold Wenglinsky, *Are Private High Schools Better Academically Than Public High Schools?* (Washington, DC: Center on Education Policy, October 10, 2007).

11. Dan Goldhaber, "Public and Private High Schools: Is School Choice an Answer to the Productivity Problem?" *Economics of Education Review* 15, no. 2 (April 1996): 93–109.

12. Christopher Lubienski and Sarah Theule Lubienski, *Charter, Private, Public Schools and Academic Achievement: New Evidence from NAEP Mathematics Data* (New York: National Center for the Study of Privatization in Education, January 2006).

13. For example, see David N. Figlio and Joe A. Stone, "School Choice and Student Performance: Are Private Schools Really Better?" (Madison: Institute for Research on Poverty, University of Wisconsin, 1997), http://www.irp.wisc.edu/publications/dps/pdfs/dp114197.pdf.

14. For example, see John Witte, Jr., et al., *The MPCP Longitudinal Educational Growth Study Second Year Report*, SCDP Milwaukee Evaluation, Report #10 (Fayetteville: School Choice Demonstration Project, University of Arkansas, March 2009).

15. Sol Stern, "Save the Catholic Schools," *City Journal*, Spring 2007.

16. "U.S. Department of Education 2011 Blue Ribbon Schools Program: Statistical Summary of National Participation," December 7, 2011.

17. Alan J. Borsuk and Sarah Carr, "Inside Choice Schools: 15 Years of Vouchers," *Milwaukee Journal Sentinel*, June 12, 2005.

18. Bruce D. Baker, "Not All Private Schools Are Created Equal," *Education Week*, August 19, 2009.

19. Domanico, *Catholic Schools in New York City*.

20. See Coleman and Hoffer, *Public and Private High Schools*; and Bryk, Holland, and Lee, *Catholic Schools and the Common Good*.

21. The normal curve distribution overlay was added by the research team; it is "appropriately scaled and has the same mean and standards deviation data."

22. All performance data are from the 2008–9 school year. For twelve schools at the fourth-grade level and fourteen schools at the eighth-grade level, no FRPL data were available for that school year, so 2009–10 FRPL levels were used (at both grade levels this represents less than 15 percent of observations). In instances where FRPL data were available for neither year, the schools were excluded. The substitution of 2009–10 data for 2008–9 data should have minimal impact on the results presented because schools' FRPL levels change little from year to year: among schools in this sample that have FRPL levels for both years, the average difference is less than 6 percentage points.

23. Data from the second diocese do not distinguish between urban and non-urban schools. However, the vast majority of its poorest schools are in urban areas.

24. In third grade the difference is 1.4 national percentile points; in grades five and seven it is 177.0 and 71.7 respectively.

Part IV

The Urban School System of the Future

Slowly, quietly, far from the public spotlight, new kinds of public institutions are emerging. They are lean, decentralized, and innovative. They are flexible, adaptable, quick to learn new ways when conditions change. They use competition, customer choice, and other nonbureaucratic mechanisms to get things done as creatively and effectively as possible. And they are our future.
—David Osborne and Ted Gaebler, *Reinventing Government*, 1992

Because of the education world's fixation on sector, our policies and politics have never come to grips with an essential fact of urban schools: The results from one sector are remarkably similar to those of the other two. Long missed or ignored, this fact is the cornerstone of this book's final section. Upon it is built a new system that properly addresses the wide variance in quality among a city's collection of schools. The tools used to construct this new system are the principles of chartering—a set of concepts turned into practices with the potential to revolutionize urban K–12 education.

Chapter 10

Characteristics of the New System

DIFFERENT STARTING POINT, DIFFERENT FINISH LINE

In important and possibly jarring ways, this study is different than similarly motivated books. Previous contributions almost always focus on how to make inner-city traditional public schools function better. As a result, there are mountains of work on teacher quality, staffing, assessments, and more. These emanate from the view that America has a serious urban *schools* problem. But as shown throughout this book, there are high-performing urban schools. The problem is that no urban area has nearly enough great schools. And, of course, all urban areas have entirely too many tragically low-performing schools.

These facts led this book in a different direction. Rather than asking how we can improve our existing collection of traditional public schools, the question here became, "Why don't we have a *system* that gets us more great schools, eradicates bad schools, and continues this cycle into the future?" This is more than a semantic reformulation of a familiar problem that will merely lead to familiar recommendations. Stark differences follow from this approach.

First, the focus here is on the system, several levels above the school itself. Second, our question suggests a process; we're not looking for some way to get better schools at a single point in time but a means of guaranteeing an adequate supply of great schools year after year. Third, many other studies give short shrift to the existence of great urban schools. Others acknowledge them and then say, "Other schools should follow their lead." In the plan offered here, great schools take on a wholly different role.

Fourth, our question doesn't presume that fixing persistently failing schools is a central task. While most studies proceed as though all or most of yesterday's schools, whatever their condition, will be tomorrow's schools, this approach is open to other possibilities. Fifth, the traditional public school district isn't an explicit part of our question. Virtually all other studies assume that the district must be the dominant actor moving forward. Sixth, our question focuses on "schools" not "traditional public schools" or even "public schools." The standard preoccupation with sector has been excised.

With these principles in place we can look anew at urban K–12 schooling and consider what needs to change. The place to start is the schools we have. In chapters 3, 6, and 9, we saw that there is great variation in the effectiveness of low-income urban schools run by each sector. A crucial insight is that the education landscape across America's cities looks largely the same. There are three overlapping sectors, each with high performers, low performers, and many in between.

The next step is to resist the urge to quibble over which sector's curve is farthest to right. That fruitless battle has gone on far too long, supported, unfortunately, by research comparing the average performance of each sector. Whatever the ordinal arrangement of any single city's curves, two critical points appear to hold across jurisdictions: Each sector is contributing schools at each level of quality, and the variation among schools within any sector is far greater than the difference between the average performance of different sectors.

That is, the difference between the best and worst district public schools is far larger than the difference between the average district public school and the average charter public school. Consequently, our focus must shift from the curves to the X-axis. We want more right-side schools and fewer left-side schools. We need a system that delivers this result continuously.

More than merely prioritizing performance over sector, this approach will also put us in position to respond when a particular sector in a given city generates unusually strong overall results, produces a disproportionate number of high- and low-performing schools, or generates schools with unusually low levels of performance variation.

Our current "system" for getting more good schools and fewer bad ones has been, in effect, efforts to push the traditional public school curve to the right: Begin by assuming that the district has a static set of schools and then try to improve those that are underperforming. To the extent those on the right are considered, they are just held up as models for others to emulate. However, this isn't how other industries behave. Elsewhere, no entity is assumed to go on forever irrespective of its quality. Persistent failures are brought to an end, great entities grow, and new entities come into being. Continuously.

The contention here is that other fields' adoption of this process isn't a coincidence. Instead, this process is *the* path for a system's continuous improvement. Similarly it has been argued here that urban public education's custom of relentlessly trying to fix persistent failures, all but ignoring high-flyers, and insufficiently taking advantage of new starts is a formula for chronic systemic underperformance.

The recommendations here simply take the lessons learned and utilized elsewhere and apply them to urban schooling. The principles of chartering will enable us to do just that by using practices already field-tested in and found compatible with public education. In other words, we must create an entirely different system for managing urban K–12 schooling.

CLOSER THAN WE THINK

Building an *entirely different* system for urban education is an audacious goal. Paul Hill and colleagues wrote that the development of a "portfolio district"—a somewhat more modest undertaking—"means rebuilding a school district from the ground up."[1] So such a dramatic proposition is susceptible to being dismissed. Everyone knows big, hoary public systems are seldom changed. They have powerful and obstinate partisans, and reformers have limited time, energy, and funding. Most would consider it unwise and impractical to take on such work.

But the plan offered here has three virtues that should quell such concerns. First, we already have the tools required. Chartering has provided the blueprints, and communities from coast to coast have been following them for two decades. Better yet, leading cities are showing how these tools can be brought to scale and combined into a coherent strategy.

In terms of practicality, the second asset may be even more important. Most proposals suggesting a complete overhaul of school systems act as though we have the luxury of starting a new system from scratch, fail to appreciate implementation challenges, and/or require enormous changes to the system we already have. The course of action recommended here is eminently feasible. For a number of urban areas, most of the shifts will be in degree and intensity not substance. Most importantly, the traditional public school district would face only one major alteration: It would lose the right to keep open its failing schools.

Third, potentially the plan's most objectionable component—the inclusion of private schools—could be omitted by those urban areas unwilling to take this step. This is not recommended, but the practices recommended here and the structures needed to carry them out could be applied to two sectors instead of three.

A WORD ABOUT THE DISTRICT

Because of its historical leading role in urban public education, the tradition-al district deserves lingering attention. Moving forward, our view of the district should be formed by two contrasting set of facts. On the one hand, we must acknowledge that for generations districts had an exclusive right to provide public schools, and they did so at an enormous scale. All major urban districts today educate thousands and thousands of students. They employ thousands of adults, have budgets in the billions, and have histories occasionally spanning a century.

Countless laws, practices, and careers were built with these arrangements in mind. Consequently, many observers still see districts *as* public education. These facts can't and shouldn't be ignored.

But on the other hand, it is now clear that the district is expendable. For the last twenty years, chartering has demonstrated that districts aren't the only entities able to deliver public education. The experience in New Or-leans, where a majority of students are educated in schools not run by the traditional system, shows that the district need not even be the dominant provider. With charter market shares in Washington, D.C., Detroit, Kansas City, and Dayton above or approaching one-third, we know this lesson is transferable.

So as we think about the future, we should be realistic about the district's standing, strengths, and weaknesses. The most important observation is that the district was not constructed to do the things identified here as essential to the new system. The district was created to operate a large, stable set of similar schools each of which is tied to a discrete geographic area and that, in combination, serve all of a city's public school students.

Districts weren't built to constantly develop different types of schools populated through parental choice. They weren't designed to continuously identify, replicate, and expand their best schools. They weren't designed to regularly close and replace failing schools. They weren't designed to author-ize others to run autonomous schools. These tasks are not in the DNA of the traditional school district.

This has been noted by Paul Hill and his colleagues at the University of Washington. In a report on the development of portfolio school districts they wrote, "Many things traditional school districts were originally built to do…are at odds with operation of schools by diverse providers and replacing schools and staff that do not perform."[2] This can be seen in recent events. Though new starts, replications, closures, and diversification have been widespread in the charter sector, most urban districts have avoided some if not all of these.

Other districts have adopted some, but generally the fit has been uncomfortable. While some districts have approved charters, many have shown themselves to be unwilling, indifferent, or hostile authorizers. While some have created new alternative schools, even occasionally contracting out for their operation, seldom do these schools have true or lasting autonomy. In the two cases where districts have most fully embraced the practices advocated here—New Orleans and New York City—major changes to the basic characteristics of the district structure came first.

In New Orleans, Hurricane Katrina decimated the district, and a new system was built with newly started charters at the fore. In New York, the school system was put under mayoral control, and a remarkably reform-minded schools leader, Joel Klein, had the authority to pursue a radically new course. In fact, it appears that no system governed by a traditional school board has ever adopted the portfolio concept.[3]

For these reasons, the district has a much-reduced place in the system recommended here. It must not be the lone school provider, and it is not assured to be the primary provider. It will not control the city's supply of schools, and another entity will address the district's highest-performing and lowest-performing schools. But because of its established place in the landscape and its current service of the preponderance of students, the district isn't discarded. Instead it is allowed to continue its primary function, operating schools, though with limits.

PILLARS OF THE NEW SYSTEM

The new system is based on five pillars designed to ensure that the city constantly maximizes its supply of great schools, minimizes its supply of poor schools, and enables families to find schools that meet their needs.

1. Great schools from all sectors will be expanded and replicated.
2. Persistently failing schools will be closed.
3. New schools will be continuously started.
4. There will be wide diversity in the schools available as well as in the entities empowered to authorize and oversee them.
5. Families can exercise choice.

The image in Figure 10.1 provides a visual representation of the principles in action. On the far right, the highest performing schools are identified and efforts are made to scale them by adding grades or enrollment or creating new campuses or schools based on the same model. All great schools, regardless of operator, will have the opportunity and the assistance needed to expand. On the far left, the most persistently low-performing schools are identified and closed (with adjustments made for failing private schools). New schools, from various sectors and with varying characteristics, continually enter the landscape.

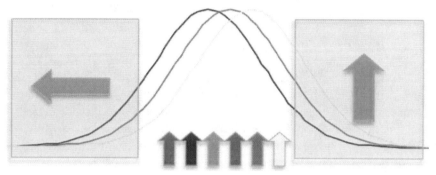

Figure 10.1

CREATING THE NEW SYSTEM

Though greater detail is provided below, the broad strokes of the system are as follows. A new entity, the Office of the Chancellor of City Schools, becomes the top K–12 education body. It is responsible for overseeing the city's entire broad portfolio of schools. Its most important function is executing the system's five basic principles.

School authorizers approve the creation of new schools, monitor school performance and legal compliance, and close failing schools. School operators, including school management organizations and the traditional public school district, are entities than run two or more schools. While school operators play key roles in the day-to-day operations of their schools, ultimately individual schools are held accountable by authorizers. Schools may associate themselves with such operators, or they may run independently.

The system depicted in Figure 10.2 should look familiar because it's similar to today's landscape in most cities. There are many different schools; some are traditional public, some are charter public, and some are private. Some schools operate independently, some are run by an operator, whether a CMO, EMO, or school district. There are authorizers to monitor the performance of some schools.

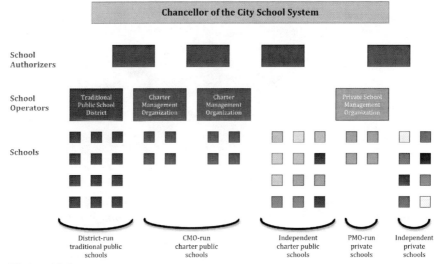

Figure 10.2

The major difference is that today's sprawling landscape would be organized into a coherent system. We would recognize that all schools are in the same business irrespective of operator and that the various pieces should function together.

This philosophical shift is operationalized via two simple changes: authorizers are placed above the school district and participating private schools, and the entire system is given leadership by the chancellor. The contours of the new system can be best explained through a description of four of its elements: the chancellor of city schools, authorizers, operators, and private schools.

CHANCELLOR OF THE CITY SCHOOL SYSTEM

The system will be led by a new office and a new top education official, the chancellor. This body will be above and work on behalf of all three sectors. This statement implies two critically important characteristics. First, by being "above" the sectors, the chancellor is *not* in the business of school operation. This office will not in any way manage schools; it will not staff schools, develop pay schedules, evaluate teachers, or anything else related to schools' daily work. Instead, the chancellor keeps the system functioning properly.

Second, by working on behalf of all three sectors, the chancellor is responsible for and is a supporter of all of the city's schools. The chancellor loves all great schools and opposes all inferior schools irrespective of which sectors they come from. Unlike those currently with the title "chancellor," for example in New York City or Washington, D.C., who serve as the head of the district, the new chancellor is not attached to a single sector. This office will have no reflexive preference for one set of schools. The office will differentiate schools based solely on their quality.

The chancellor administers the city's extensive portfolio of schools by ensuring that the five pillars are executed. The goal is to make certain that families have access to the schools they need. This has at least three elements: performance, diversity, and geography. Schools must be academically superior, they must be sufficiently varied to meet the wide needs of the city's children, and they must be arrayed across the geography so neighborhoods have access to the grade spans and programs needed.

This is a system very different from today's, which has handled one of these requirements reasonably well and the other two miserably. By assigning students to schools by their home addresses and providing a primary and secondary school to each community, the system assured that families had access to public schools. But when one or more of that community's schools was of poor quality, the system had no alternative but to try to improve it. If the school continued to fail, students would still be assigned to it. Furthermore, residence-based assignments fail to acknowledge that many students are poorly served by a one-size-fits-all approach.

The duties of the chancellor elevate the place of quality and diversity while guaranteeing access. The result can be thought of as "managed fluidity" or a "publicly organized schools marketplace." The chancellor provides the foundation of this system by carefully integrating three activities: replications/expansions, closures, and new starts. Louisiana's former state superintendent, Paul Pastorek, used the term "harvester of high-quality schools"— launching new schools, evaluating existing schools, nurturing successful schools, closing failing ones—to describe the state's role in helping reconstruct New Orleans' school system.[4]

The chancellor is charged with identifying the city's highest performing schools and enabling them to do more. This could include starting additional campuses, expanding enrollment, or adding new grade levels. Heretofore, traditional districts did little to nothing to scale their best schools, and excelling charters have shouldered the burdens of expansion themselves. Since it's in the public's interest to scale great schools, the public system should facilitate this process. Though it is too soon to tell the full range of activities that could be part of the chancellor's arsenal on this front, our charter experience suggests several types of initiatives.

Growing schools will need assistance accessing facilities, writing business plans, developing management systems, and recruiting human capital. The chancellor's responsibilities could also include ensuring that families have access to the types of information needed to make wise choices. This could include publishing school directories, sponsoring school fairs, and disseminating robust school report cards. Currently, in choice-friendly cities, like Minneapolis–St. Paul and the District of Columbia, this work is undertaken by a range of government and nonprofit organizations with little coordination.

The chancellor should also have the authority to help excellent schools navigate or change laws, regulations, and other policies that inhibit growth. The leaders of a number of the highest performing CMOs believe that "cumbersome or duplicative policies and procedures provide disincentives for replication." These include rules related to charter renewals, school governance, and authorizer jurisdiction.[5] As more high-quality seats become available, the chancellor will work with authorizers to phase out the system's most persistently struggling schools. After having sufficient opportunity to improve, schools that remain underperforming lose their right to operate. Closure decisions will be based on two sets of criteria.

First, each school will have a clear and thorough performance contract with an authorizer. Consistent inability to reach achievement targets and other agreed-upon standards (e.g., safety, financial, management) will make the school susceptible to closure. Though these determinations will be made primarily by authorizers, it will be the responsibility of the chancellor to choreograph closures based on the second set of criteria—the availability of better schools.

Closures only improve achievement in the short-term if affected students are able to transfer to higher-performing schools.[6] As the chancellor determines when a school ought to close and whether it should be immediate or gradual, she will weigh several factors. These include whether the community has access to nearby schools that are stronger and have space, if good schools elsewhere in the city are able to start a new campus in the affected area, and/or whether other entities are ready to launch a new school in the neighborhood.

New starts are the chancellor's final major area of activity. Though chartering has flourished, in most urban areas the starting of new schools has been organic. Those interested take the initiative, develop a proposal, and submit it to a passive authorizer. But new schools are in the system's best interest; they are essential for ongoing improvement. So the system should play an active role in new starts. While authorizers will remain disinterested umpires—calling balls and strikes on applications—the chancellor will facilitate the development of new schools.

Primary activities in this area will include recruiting and providing assistance to existing organizations to develop schools; seeding new organizations to develop schools; and recruiting school providers from other cities. The chancellor might also help launch independent school support organizations, such as resource centers and technical assistance providers. The chancellor ought to be given a wide berth to enable her to adequately address pressing but previously unconsidered issues that arise.

For example, Baltimore found that since some school names have important historical significance, closures could be especially difficult in some communities. So it developed a system for temporarily "retiring" a name and giving it priority when a new school is developed.[7]

Though managing and integrating replications, closures, and new starts will comprise the bulk of the chancellor's work, other responsibilities will also be important. She should be responsible for determining which private schools are allowed to participate in the public system (private schools are considered fully below). This would include setting eligibility criteria, providing accreditation, and monitoring compliance. The chancellor should also have control over the system's stock of facilities, in order to ensure that schools have access to suitable buildings (also considered below).

More generally, she will work to maintain diversity among school providers and school authorizers. A wide array of quality schools provides the greatest likelihood that students' needs are met, and a wide array of quality authorizers provides the greatest likelihood that such schools have the opportunity to launch and thrive.

Should the city have a surfeit of excellent schools hoping to expand or high-quality entities hoping to begin new schools, the chancellor, in collaboration with authorizers, will have authority to manage the circumstances. She would use her discretion to adjudicate competing considerations (such as a provider's preference to only start schools in a certain area or a neighborhood's need for a specific type of program) and address emerging challenges (e.g., a brewing shortage of elementary schools or the growing homogenization of available programs).

Though the chancellor's office could be established in a number of ways, ideally it would be created under state law with the chancellor appointed by the mayor. Such arrangements would give the office legal standing and a modicum of independence while still embedding the work within the larger city government. Numerous variations are possible, though: The office could be housed under the state education agency, the chancellor could be appointed by the governor, or an official advisory board might be developed.

In total, while the chancellor will not operate schools, she will keep the system fluid, responsive, high-performing, and self-improving by facilitating and managing starts, closures, and expansions; guaranteeing diversity; and enabling choice.

AUTHORIZERS

An authorizer is an entity with the power to accept and render judgments on applications for the creation of new public schools, develop contracts with approved school providers, and hold schools to account for their performance. The development of charter authorizers made sense. Their existence allowed the different functions of school operation and school oversight to be separated. It also enabled a logical process for starting new public schools, developing transparent performance contracts, and closing schools not up to snuff.

In the new system, the role of authorizers in the charter sector would remain unchanged. Existing charters would still have contracts with authorizers. The relationship between some charters and authorizers would continue to be mediated by a charter management organization that operates several schools, while other charters would interface with the authorizer directly, eschewing CMO management. Those hoping to start new charters would still apply to authorizers, and authorizers would monitor charter performance.

The only substantive difference for charters would be the chancellor's collaborative role in helping to manage the development of new schools, replicate great schools, and close poor schools. A major curiosity of the current system is that school authorization is still confined to the charter sector. The proposal here would expand authorizers across the urban K–12 landscape—meaning the other two sectors would be included.

First, all district public schools would become accountable to a school authorizer. While the district would retain its right to own and operate its schools as it saw fit, it would play the same role as a CMO. That is, it would be a school operator, running schools and serving as an intermediary between its schools and the authorizer. But each traditional public school would have a contract with an authorizer. The authorizer would hold the school accountable for meeting its academic, financial, and management targets. If the school consistently failed to perform adequately, the authorizer would have the power to close it.

In the new system, authorizers would also play an important role in the private schools sector. More attention is paid below to the participation of private schools in the new system, but authorizers would have virtually the same responsibilities to each sector. Each participating private school (private schools would choose to participate, not be forced) would have a performance contract with an authorizer, and schools could interact with the authorizer directly or be operated by a private school management organization.

The only major difference is that an authorizer could not close a private school. It could, however, remove the school from the public system, meaning the private school would lose its eligibility for public funding and the other benefits of the public system. Such a school would then go on in the same manner as private schools currently function; it would charge tuition and depend on philanthropy, adhere to basic safety and accreditation standards, and be governed by the market.

In total, every school that is part of the public system—meaning all traditional public schools, all charter public schools, and all participating private schools—would be monitored by an authorizer. Authorizers would differentiate schools based on their quality, not on their sector. Authorizers would allow schools serving their students well to continue operating, and they would close failing public schools and remove failing private schools from the public system.

Currently, many entities act as school authorizers, including mayors, state departments of education, nonprofits, and single-purpose authorizers. However, in the future state policymakers could significantly expand this pool. In many locations, the district, in addition to operating its own schools, also authorizes charters. This has often been a troubled venture. It places the district in the awkward position of regulating its competition and forcing the district to undertake activities far outside of its core competency.

In the system recommended here, the district would no longer be able to serve as both school operator and authorizer. A pitcher can't call his own balls and strikes. A prosecutor can't render verdicts in his own trials. So too, the roles of participant and evaluator must be separated in urban public education. Those running schools can't have the final say on their duration.

In the majority of cases, the district, when forced to choose, would opt to continue as a schools operator. Hypothetically, it could shift into the role of school authorizer, though this would require ending virtually all of its practices and terminating its current relationship with its schools: It would no longer hire principals, purchase textbooks, manage bus routes, and so forth. If a district became a full-time operator, it would still have the authority to run its schools in a wide variety of ways. It could micromanage, have a hands-off approach, or something in between. How it goes about this is its own affair.

The system would have no predetermined preference for how the district interfaced with its schools; in the eyes of authorizers and the chancellor this is immaterial. Schools would be evaluated solely on their quality. Ends, not means, matter most in the urban school system of the future.

SCHOOL OPERATORS

A consequence of the advent of authorizers was the rise of school operators—non-district entities that run public schools. In the early days of chartering, an operator was merely the school itself, or more specifically the nonprofit organization contractually empowered to conduct the school's business. But over time, as replications and expansions emerged, new entities began overseeing more than one school.

Now known as charter management organizations and education management organizations (CMOs and EMOs), these groups take advantage of economies of scale to facilitate the operation of a network of schools. For example, a CMO might provide a common curriculum to all of its schools; conduct professional development for all of its teachers; or centrally manage hiring, payroll, and benefits. In practice, school management organizations have taken a number or forms: some tightly manage their schools, others use a light touch; some operate a dozen or more schools, while others oversee only two or three.

This variation is possible because of the superstructure of the charter concept: Outputs, not inputs, matter most. While these organizations play an unquestionably important role, the pertinent relationship remains between the school and the authorizer, and that relationship is driven by questions of quality. If the school succeeds, it continues; if it fails, it is subject to closure. The practices of a school's operator are means, not ends, so they can vary.

In the system recommended here, organizations running charter schools will remain essentially unchanged. The chancellor will help new organizations get started, help great organizations grow, and work with these entities to ensure that all neighborhoods throughout the city have an array of high-quality options. But this will be a collaborative effort, and such cooperation will typically be at the strategic level. Tactically, these organizations will work like they do today—hiring teachers, recruiting students, developing assessment systems, and so on.

It is into this increasingly recognized role that the school district will settle. Rather than maintaining its hegemony over public schooling—whereby it controls and speaks for all aspects of public education—the district will become solely the operator of a great number of public schools. In the future, it can be thought of as a DMO ("district management organization"), a counterpart to CMOs and EMOs. Like other operators, the DMO can run its schools as it chooses. It will continue to have discretion over the employment of its central staff and teacher corps, the provision of services to its schools, and so forth.

It can even continue to run schools in different ways, for example operating specialty or magnet schools or maintaining contracts with independent providers to operate various aspects of schools' programs. For as long as the district's schools operate, it owns them as it does now. But "as long as" is the operative phrase, for the district's schools will not be guaranteed immortality, and the district will not have the final say on its schools' life spans.

Just as charter public schools operated by CMOs and EMOs have performance agreements with authorizers, so too will traditional public schools operated by the DMO. Kennedy Elementary, the neighborhood public school, will have a contractual relationship with an authorizer. So will the city's STEM magnet school and the innovative public school specializing in the performing arts. Hopefully, all of these schools will thrive; but if any fails to meet its obligations to its students, it will be subject to closure.

A corollary is that the district will no longer be able to claim the mantle of "educator of last resort," the entity responsible for ensuring that all students have a public school to attend. Historically, while an authorizer could close a charter and not worry about the other options available, the district had no such luxury. This safety-net role, however, proved monumentally problematic, allowing districts to keep failing schools open and enjoy a cosseted place in the landscape. In the new system, the chancellor has the responsibility for maintaining the supply of schools by working with authorizers and operators to maintain a robust portfolio.

A major implication of the shift from public education leviathan to DMO is that the size and market share of the district will vary from city to city, and within each city it will vary from year to year. If the DMO is able to run highly effective schools, its portfolio will grow as its strong performers continue on and its best performers replicate and expand. But if it runs a stable of persistently failing schools, its footprint will shrink as its schools are phased out. Depending on the quality of its schools, the district could be the dominant provider or work itself out of business.

The DMO has no inherent right to run all public schools or even a majority of public schools; indeed, it has no right to run *any* public schools. The district's station will be determined by its effectiveness.

PRIVATE SCHOOLS

Other nations have shown that private schools can be part of a comprehensive K–12 system. Integrating our private schools into the new public system should begin with the same principles applied to the other sectors. First, each participating private school will be required to have a performance contract with an authorizer. Second, a private school's good standing depends on its ability to meet the academic and other provisions in its agreement.

Third, though the legal relationship will be between a school and an authorizer, there is a role for the private school equivalent of a CMO, an entity that helps operate more than one private school, here named a PMO ("private school management organization"). A likely candidate for a PMO would be a Catholic diocese, an established body with a long history of overseeing a number of related private schools. Or a large diocese with schools spread across a large geographic area may have a designated office that manages only its inner-city schools.

Other options exist. Other faiths run multiple schools in some cities, and occasionally these schools are linked. So a set of Lutheran or Friends schools might be managed by a central office. It is not uncommon for a number of independent private schools in a city to form an association. Such an alliance might include religious and secular private schools. Though the Cristo Rey and NativityMiguel networks are support organizations for like schools, these and similar groups could serve as management organizations. Finally, a city might start a new PMO to help operate several private schools or seed, develop, and launch new private schools.

There are, however, three unique challenges to including private schools. But each can be addressed. The first issue is deciding which private schools to include initially. This duty should ultimately rest in the hands of the chancellor, though other city leaders and state policymakers might weigh in. Though there are many possibilities, they can be thought of as falling along a continuum. A loose process would establish minimal barriers to entrance, allowing virtually all private schools to participate initially. The lone criteria might be accreditation from an established body and/or recognition by the state.

To set tighter criteria, additional factors could be considered: A minimum number of years of operation, proof of strong academic performance, or indicators of proper financial management might be required. An even stricter process might include only high-performing private schools in geographic areas of need or might set a ceiling on the total number of private schools eligible to participate. An extremely restrictive option would only include secular private schools. Whatever the decision on the front end, it will be mediated by the second issue: addressing the lowest-performing private schools.

Persistently under-performing public schools can be closed, but private schools have a constitutional right to operate so long as they are privately financed. So the city can't unilaterally close failing private schools. Ideally, the chancellor and authorizers would ensure that performance contracts for private schools were identical in most material ways to those of public schools. This would mean, for example, requiring private schools to administer standardized assessments, meet proficiency and graduation benchmarks, and report on key financial practices.

If a participating private school consistently failed to meet its contract's specifications, the authorizer and chancellor might remove it from the public system. The private school could still operate as it had in the old system— accepting students, running on tuition payments—but it would no longer be eligible for public funding, assistance from the chancellor's office, or other benefits of the system.

Various locations could decide on different levels of flexibility. One state might decide that participation requires the administration of the state assessment while another might decide that private schools could administer a different standardized assessment. One state might choose to set minimal rules on teacher qualifications while another would require participating private schools to use only licensed teachers.

For officials attempting to devise the best system, a wise approach for simultaneously recognizing the public nature of the system and respecting private schools' historical autonomy would be to begin with the freedoms granted to charters under state law and then provide additional flexibility as warranted. For instance, the strong performance of many religious schools may be a consequence of practices emanating from faith, so it would be imprudent to force schools to make drastic changes in these areas.

If done properly, allowing religious practices in schools participating in a public system is wholly consistent with the U.S. Constitution. Such discussions should be part of the process of addressing the third challenge of integrating private schools: funding. To incentivize private schools to join the system, enable them to succeed, and justify the changes they'll be forced to make, participation must merit public financial support. This could be accomplished in three ways.

Optional Participation

From the public's point of view, private schools have much to offer. So the public—as represented by their elected officials and other policymakers—should develop a sensible process for integrating these schools into the broader public system. The explanation below offers a plan for not only accomplishing this, but also doing so in a way consistent with the findings revealed and principles endorsed throughout this book. Moreover, this plan would evaluate and treat private schools no differently than public schools. The result then, from the public's perspective, is a comprehensive and coherent system.

But private schools have a long history outside of the public system, and many of these schools might prefer to keep it that way. They might enjoy the prestige that accompanies fully private status; they might worry that excessive entanglement with the state would compromise their mission or practices. Others, however, might welcome an invitation into the public system. They may see the private tag as a liability or simply unreflective of their work. They may see the benefits of participation as far greater than the potential downsides.

For these reasons, the plan offered here is optional for private schools. They would not be required to take part. They would be free to carry on as is. The choice is theirs to make.

On the upside, the new system could offer them public funding—certainly a boon to schools relying on tuition but serving the poor. It could help them a find a facility—welcome news for those in undersized, aging, or deteriorating buildings. It could provide them assistance in scaling up to serve more families and neighborhood—a pleasant enticement for those committed to helping as many disadvantaged kids as possible. But participation would probably mean a number of changes in the way they assess their students, the way they report their performance, and more. The exact contours would be determined by the policymakers in each city, and these are bound to vary in sundry ways.

Figure 10.3

Currently, the most sensible route would be through a large-scale scholarship program. The city would set a private school per-pupil allotment. Each student choosing a participating private school would receive that amount, which would cover that student's school expenses. Students would gain access to more schools, participating private schools would have a stable stream of income; and, per *Zelman,* faith-based schools in non-Blaine states could maintain their religious elements.

Ideally, the city would already have a student-based funding system whereby every school in the public system would be funded at an amount equal to the product of its enrollment and the per-pupil allotment. This would allow student enrollment to shift naturally between schools and sectors. If P.S. 32 saw a student surge while St. John's lost enrollment, each school's funding level would adjust appropriately.

A second option is a scholarship tax credit program. The city could offer tax credits to individuals and corporations that contribute to a private schools funding pool. This money would then be allocated to participating private schools in amounts reflecting their enrollment. This method also passes constitutional muster and (based on the experience of extant state-level programs) it has the added benefit of generating less political animosity than vouchers. It would also generate a relatively reliable stream of funding and enable private schools to maintain their practices.

On the downside, decreased private contributions would depress the number of students able to enroll in participating private schools. It would also continue to support the notion that the private sector is a separate system.

A final option would be for a city to develop a simple funding system whereby every student is allocated a certain level of funding; every participating school then receives from the government that amount times the number of students enrolled. The only difference between this system and a large-scale voucher program is that, in this case, some amount of money would flow from the government directly to some number of private schools (instead of that money first flowing through families).

This system would maximize parental choice, fluidity, transparency, and equity. However, it is unconstitutional under current jurisprudence: Public funding reaching religious schools must be directed there by families.

A city could develop such a system and then litigate before the courts, arguing that there is no meaningful difference between it and a permissible voucher plan. In both systems a private school receives government aid based solely on the number of students sent to it by their parents. The only variation is in the proposed system money travels from the government to the private school and in the voucher system money makes a brief pit stop at a student's home—a distinction without a difference.

Regardless of the system selected, the city would still need to make other decisions about smaller but still nontrivial matters. These include the amount of money allocated in per-pupil aid, whether amounts will vary based on school level, whether amounts will vary based on student needs, whether private school allotments would be means-tested, and whether private schools outside of the city's lines can participate.

ADDITIONAL ISSUES TO CONSIDER

To make the most out of the new system and facilitate the transition, the following—surely *not* exhaustive—list of issues should be considered.

Facilities: Today's patchwork system of multiple unaffiliated sectors has led to suboptimal and unwieldy facilities arrangements. In many cities, the district has a large stock of underutilized buildings, charters struggle to find suitable quarters, and the private sector suffers both problems and more. If the new system is to be comprehensive, coordinated and capable of managing frequent new starts, expansions, and closures, cities must develop a more sensible process.[8] They might transfer the stock of existing city-owned school buildings to the chancellor's office or another entity and empower that organization to offer leases to school providers, conduct maintenance, purchase new buildings, and sell excess properties.

Funding: Cities should consider moving to a more equitable, simplified, and transparent process for funding schools. Since all participating schools will be equal partners, they should receive comparable support. These funding arrangements should also be sufficiently nimble to support a system where students move between schools and the portfolio changes frequently. One option is a fully portable, student-based system whereby a certain amount of funding follows each student to the participating school of his choice. School operators (DMO, CMOs, EMOs, and PMOs) could then charge schools for their services. Since there are currently prohibitions on federal aid reaching private schools directly, cities should consider how to address the disparities that result.

Collective Bargaining Agreements (CBAs): Labor contracts and the unions who negotiate them have been purposely absent from these pages. Just as the recommended system assiduously avoids tendentiousness with regard to sector, it has no inherent bias for or against labor contracts. Instead, they are seen as inputs, potential contributors (maybe positive, maybe negative) to school quality.

Since the system evaluates schools based solely on their quality, the effects of unionization on student performance will naturally reveal itself: If the preponderance of shuttered schools have strict contracts, that will speak volumes; so too if the majority of high-performing schools are unionized.

The union question should resolve itself as long as one principle is followed: No currently non-unionized school should be forced to unionize and all newly started schools should have the opportunity to be non-unionized. So a state law requiring the district to negotiate with bargaining units need not be changed initially. If the DMO's schools flounder, the system's leadership, worried that its portfolio will diminish, will have incentive to renegotiate its CBA if it is deemed a problem.

If there is no guarantee that the replacement for a shuttered unionized school will be unionized, the union—lest the size of its membership deteriorate—will have incentive to renegotiate the CBA. In this way, contracts can become a force for quality: With the right policies, both labor and management are compelled by self-interest to develop agreements that produce high-performing schools. If an existing or newly created school chooses to unionize, that is its prerogative. A contract should not be foisted upon any school, but nor should it be proscribed.

But in order to drive quality, policymakers should prohibit all new contracts from covering more than one school. If management and labor understand that the fate of their school and their jobs ride solely on the school's performance, contracts will support quality. But if a contract guarantees those working in School A a job in School B, School A's employees may be less alarmed by their school's declining quality and the prospect of closure, and School B's quality could be compromised if it is required to employ staff it would rather not.

CONCLUSION

This chapter's recommendations are built on widely held principles and uncomplicated empirical findings.

Disadvantaged kids deserve great schools. Even among their lowest income schools, each sector has wide variations in quality. School quality should matter more to us than school sector. There should be a wide array of education options, and families should be able to exercise choice. High-performing schools should be able to expand. Persistently low-performing schools should be brought to an end. New entrants should be welcomed into the fold.

Hopefully, the draw of this chapter is that we can operationalize these findings and values via the available principles of chartering. By expanding the work of authorizers, reconsidering the role of school operators, embracing school replications, making greater use of performance contracts, closing more failing schools, and developing more new schools, we can create a dynamic, responsive, high-performing, and self-improving school system for America's urban schools.

To a skeptic, these ideas may appear fanciful. The policy world is crowded with high-minded, mellifluous, but completely impractical proposals for solving social challenges. But this book's last chapter offers a final attraction, a compelling argument for why pursuing these recommendations is not just theoretically in the best interest of city students, but also a cause well worth the effort and energy. The revolution has already begun.

NOTES

1. Paul Hill, et al., *Portfolio School Districts for Big Cities*, Interim Report (Bothell: Center for Reinventing Public Education, University of Washington, October 2009).

2. Hill, et al., *Portfolio School Districts for Big Cities*.

3. Hill, et al., *Portfolio School Districts for Big Cities.*

4. Paul Tough, "A Teachable Moment," *The New York Times Magazine*, August 14, 2008.

5. Laura Bloomberg and Joe Nathan, "Achieving Excellence at Scale: State Support for High-Performing Charter School Expansion," NGA Center for Best Practices Issue Brief (Washington, DC: National Governors Association, April 15, 2009).

6. Marisa de la Torre and Julia Gwynne, *When Schools Close: Effects on Displaced Students in Chicago Public Schools* (Chicago: Consortium on Chicago School Research, October 2009).

7. Baltimore City Public Schools, *Expanding Great Options SY 2010: Reviewing Schools to Maximize Success for Students*, April 2009.

8. See also pages 23–24 in Hill, et al., *Portfolio School Districts for Big Cities*.

Chapter 11

Finishing the Job

The goal is to have a portfolio of schools that provide different options to every student in the city. But every single one of them needs to be an effective option.

—Andres Alonso, CEO, Baltimore City Public Schools
Baltimore Sun, January 3, 2010[1]

Part of my job is to make sure that all kids get a great education, and it doesn't matter whether that's in charter, parochial or public schools.

—Michelle Rhee, former chancellor, District of Columbia Public Schools
New York Times, February 27, 2009[2]

It is not about a great schools system; it is about a system of great schools.

—Joel Klein, former chancellor, New York City Public Schools
National Charter Schools Conference, June 23, 2009[3]

At its core, this book is an attempt to replace our terribly broken system of urban K–12 schooling while protecting the principles of public education; it's a study of how to reform the church while keeping the faith. The new system proposed here has a number of distinguishing characteristics. It places school quality above all else. It envisions a diversity of educational options operated by a wide array of providers. It empowers parents with choice. It is agnostic about school sector. Most importantly, it requires an entirely new method of managing a portfolio of schools over time, one that generates dynamism and continuous improvement.

Despite these significant departures from today's delivery system, this proposal preserves the heart of public education. In the new system, schools will continue to be fully accessible, tuition-free, publicly funded, and publicly accountable.

The three quotations above serve as the departure point for our final tour of this new system. Combined, they provide the framework for the two arguments of this chapter. The first is that this new system absolutely can be made real. In a number of cities, its foundation has already been laid and the framing has begun. Several prominent urban school leaders are openly embracing its principles and their teams are animating them every day.

The statements nicely adumbrate the system's contours: high-quality options, sector agnosticism, and portfolio management. Moreover, that these leaders—the primary stewards of public education in their respective cities during their tenures—openly support these types of changes powerfully underscores that it's not heretical to alter a wayward church; it's a demonstration of devotion to the underlying faith.

The second argument is that despite its taking root, this new system still needs careful cultivation if it is to fully flourish. Its ascendancy is far from inevitable. Though Klein, Rhee, Alonso, and others have made important advancements, no city has yet adopted all of the system's essential characteristics. And there is no reason to believe that this system will organically materialize in any location without thoughtful, sustained effort.

Despite the extraordinarily encouraging direction implied by the quotations, facts on the ground indicate that the concepts they advocate are still a distance from detailed game plans. In the nation's capital, there is still no strategy for integrating the three sectors. In Baltimore, it's still not clear how the city will manage its portfolio to guarantee a diversity of effective options. In the Big Apple, it's not apparent what exactly that great system actually is.

These two arguments may seem incongruous: this new system is on the way but its fate is still very much in doubt. But there is a point in every potential revolution's gestation when its momentum has an equal chance of accelerating to an unstoppable speed and grounding to a halt. This is that moment for this possible renaissance for urban public education.

In each of the four sections to follow, a fundamental characteristic of the new system is considered. The section details the major progress already underway and then describes the limits of that progress and how and why the system advocated here can break through the remaining barriers. In other words, each section is both a logbook of the journey to date and a set of future directions for one component of the urban school system of the future.

FROM DISTRICT-CENTERED TO SCHOOL-CENTERED

Possibly the most portentous shift afoot is the growing realization that we must reassess the role of the current system's core—the district. The advent of chartering caused the first cracks in the district's foundation by demonstrating that it mustn't be the owner and operator of all public schools. The proliferation of new operators and the expansion of non-district public schools now force us to wonder about the proper role for the district in the new landscape. That is, when it was the monopoly provider it had to be the driver of all activity. That is no longer the case.

As a result, a fundamental shift has occurred. The world increasingly, and accurately, thinks of a city's K–12 education system as a collection of diverse schools, not as a single, dominant administrative unit. This is the reason why the term "portfolio of schools" has become a staple of the education lexicon. It is also the reason why more and more leaders are drawing a distinction between a "school system" and a "system of schools."

Joel Klein was the primary force behind this invaluable change in language: "The first and most important thing about the work we do in New York: It is not about a great schools system; it is about a system of great schools."[4] This is far more than semantics. It encapsulates the shift from a district-centered to a school-centered approach and the resulting new way of thinking about reform, namely managing the portfolio using the strategies outlined in chapter 7. Indeed, a Klein deputy described the district's "new schools strategy" as the key to moving toward a system of great individual schools and away from a great school system.[5]

This language and the beliefs motivating it have spread like wildfire. Philadelphia's 2009 strategic plan was called "Imagine 2014: Building a System of Great Schools." It included plans to increase options, open new schools, and close failing schools. A 2008 report by Tulane University on post-Katrina New Orleans described the landscape similarly: "Because schools no longer function as a single school system, it is now more accurate to refer to public schools in New Orleans as a "system of schools."[6] Paul Pastorek used the Recovery School District to create a network of independent schools to replace the city's dysfunctional district.[7]

This school-centered approach has enabled these cities and a number of others to truly begin portfolio management. But in most locations, lasting progress will be stymied by the continued reliance on the district. That is, cities have mistakenly moved to a school-centered approach while maintaining the district as the dominant actor. In Baltimore and Chicago all public schools are still run or authorized by the district, and in Philadelphia most are. In New York City, the district has positioned itself as the portfolio manager. In these cities and many more, the district is the owner and operator of many or most new schools.

These are serious problems for a number of reasons. In order for there to be true diversity in school options, there must be diversity in school authorizers. Options will always be constrained if a single entity is in charge of deciding who gets to run schools. Moreover, the district-authorizer model compromises the dynamism of the system by allowing the district to regulate its competition. Furthermore, since urban districts were created to be school operators and have functioned in that role for decades, we have no reason to believe they can transition to the role of able portfolio managers.

Finally, empowering districts with these duties and allowing them to create and run the majority of new schools jeopardizes the sustainability of change. Unless these powers are distributed to a range of entities, an unfortunate change in the district's leadership would be calamitous. The district could cease chartering independent schools, take back control of the autonomous schools it had created, stop closures and replications, and more. All progress could be rolled back.

The proper path forward is to pair the new school-centered approach with the diminution of the district's role as outlined in the previous chapter. The district must be solely a school operator—not an authorizer or portfolio manager, not the guaranteed preeminent player in the landscape. The urban school system of the future must have diversity among operators and authorizers. All schools must be evaluated and treated equally; that is, similarly subject to the strategies in chapter 7. A single-purpose portfolio manager, unencumbered by the responsibility of running or authorizing schools, must independently guide the system.

THE PROLIFERATION OF CHOICE

Unlike the relatively recent changes in views about the district, the expansion of parental choice has been gaining steam for decades. More than twenty years ago, scholar Joe Nathan noted that public school choice had strong bipartisan support among the nation's political leaders, including then-President George H.W. Bush, then-Democratic Governors Perpich, Clinton, Dukakis, and Blanchard, and then-GOP governors Alexander, Kean, and Thompson.[8]

Options grew swiftly, enabling more parents to choose the right school for their children. According to federal figures, between 1993 and 2007, the percentage of children in their assigned neighborhood public schools fell from 80 percent to 73 percent.[9] Though charter schools enroll more than two million students, the expansion of homeschooling also contributed to this trend. More than 1.5 million students were homeschooled in 2007, nearly twice as many as in 1999.[10]

There are many reasons why elected officials and parents have embraced greater choice. The most obvious is that individuals exercise choice in countless parts of their lives and expect similar opportunities when it comes to educating their children. Some have argued that choice helps schools improve because it contributes to the construction of the kind of school climate that supports academic success.[11] Some have found that attendance is higher and dropout rates lower in public schools that students have selected.[12]

Education leaders may be growing fonder of choice because of its positive effects on parents. Research on the D.C. Opportunity Scholarship Program found that once acclimated to choice, parents become better, more selective choosers for their children. The study also found that parents' high satisfaction with the program was a function, "first and foremost," of their new ability to exercise choice.[13] Similar findings have been reported in Baltimore.[14] The *Baltimore Sun* noted, "Data released by the school system show parents and students appear to be quickly adapting, becoming savvy shoppers who pick as their first choice the highest-performing, safest schools while eschewing the least successful."[15]

In Milwaukee, more options via charters and vouchers have expanded family knowledge: Families not only understand the options available to them, they also seek schools with strong reputations, especially those with an expressed commitment to college preparation.[16] A study of New Jersey found that parents primarily choose charters based on their academic effectiveness.[17]

So there's strong cause to suspect that choice will continue to expand. In Philadelphia, the "Office of Charter, Partnerships, and New Schools" is responsible for "expanding and supporting high quality public school choice."[18] New York City has a dedicated "Office of Portfolio Development" that creates new schools to provide students more and better options.[19] In Baltimore, the goal of the district's 2009 strategic plan was "to provide parents with a range of education options to meet their child's need."[20]

But there are also several reasons to tend to this expansion carefully. As chapter 2 discussed, choice and competition alone haven't caused our traditional public schools to radically improve; absent a sensible overarching system, choice isn't a panacea. Also, not all options are of high quality; a system must be in place to address those failing to educate students. Some cities continue to have too few options; most cities still exclude private schools; and all cities lack laws, regulations, and policies to ensure that all schools are treated equitably. Finally, even in cities where options are many, some neighborhoods don't have access to sufficient schools or schools that meet their students' needs.

Though incremental changes in choice have taken place, they've lacked a broader organizing policy framework. The policy debate has failed to generate the kind of dynamic "managed-choice" system needed. As scholar Charles Glenn wrote in 1989 in words still fitting today, "Choice seems to be considered a matter of 'all or nothing,' reduced to the stark choice between social engineering and a free-for-all. But surely there are options in education between statism and libertarianism, and policy-makers should develop them carefully."[21]

The system offered here takes this middle path. It will encompass all three sectors, immediately expanding choice. Quality control will be increased by making each school sign a performance contract with an authorizer, which is empowered to close low performers. The chancellor will use her extensive authority over new starts, replications, expansions, and more to ensure that families have access to high-quality options that meet the needs of their children.

CHURNING THE SCHOOLS PORTFOLIO

Arguably the most significant trend is the growing churn in urban school portfolios. Increasingly, new starts and closures are changing cities' schools landscapes from year to year. The charter sector has driven the explosion of new schools. Charters now exist in all of the nation's twenty largest cities, and in nearly all of its fifty largest cities. In most of these locations, chartering has led to the creation of significant numbers of new schools, whether Boston, Baltimore, and Philadelphia in the East; San Francisco, Phoenix, and Houston in the West; New Orleans, Miami, and Atlanta in the South; or Chicago, Detroit, and Milwaukee in the Midwest.

But a number of traditional urban districts have also launched new school initiatives, including New York City, Chicago, Philadelphia, Los Angeles, and Baltimore. There was once an aversion to placing closures in an urban system's toolbox. Some opposed closures for political or philosophical reasons while others thought they were unworkable at scale. But a closure policy needn't be sudden, heartless, and comprehensive; it can be careful, empathetic, and nuanced. Cities are finding ways to make it an integral part of their activities.

Closures are, of course, a central component of the charter model. But in a number of major cities, including Washington, D.C., Chicago, Philadelphia, and New York City, system heads are closing their very lowest performers.[22]

Paul Pastorek, Louisiana's former state superintendent of education, provided an excellent description of this approach and its consequences. He said that if a school continues to fail after receiving support, "then you pull the plug and bring in a new provider or an experienced provider. Over a period of five or six years, ten at the most, we'll have nothing but high-quality operators in our city."[23] In a document explaining the alterations to its portfolio, the Baltimore district wrote, "Ultimately, programs that are not working for our kids were recommended for closure while thriving programs were recommended for expansion."[24]

Best, some cities are becoming increasingly sophisticated about managing churn. By coordinating efforts with school operators, service providers, and others, cities can choreograph new starts, expansions, and closures to help ensure that students always have schools to attend and that those schools are of increasing quality. This trend shows no signs of abating. Both components are building steam among education leaders. The other trends discussed—the growing recognition that the system must change and that choice has invaluable benefits—may make churn more manageable and less disquieting to parents and policymakers in the years to come.

But as with the other trends, the churning process needs guidance if it is to help revolutionize urban schooling. For some cities, closures are primarily an economic strategy not a quality one. After stating that a round of twenty-nine closures would help improve student achievement, the head of Detroit schools conceded, "This is a financial issue. None of us want any schools to close."[25] Too many cities still lack sufficient new options and avoid closures. Often this is because of a district's unwillingness to launch new schools. But it can also be the result of poor policies, inadequate human or financial capital, and deficient authorizers.

But probably the biggest problem with churn as it now stands is the shocking lack of coordination in most cities. In areas with non-district authorizers, new charters can be started and failing charters can be closed without any discussion with the district. A district might start a new school with a particular focus in a specific neighborhood when a new charter with the same program and target area is slated to open on the same day. A number of private schools might close their doors without any advance notice to the district or charter authorizer.

The new system is constructed to ensure both that churn occurs and that it is carefully managed. A wide array of organizations will be empowered to start new and different programs. Authorizers will see to it that high-quality applications turn into schools and that low-performing schools are shuttered. And the chancellor will orchestrate new starts, closures, replications and expansions with geography, grade spans, timing, program diversity, and more in mind. Though the portfolio of schools will be ever-changing, the process will be carefully coordinated so scarce resources are used properly and the system stably meets the needs of families.

INTEGRATING THE THREE SECTORS

The final trend is growing agnosticism about school sector. Though some have jealously limited their affection to traditional public schools, this is an increasingly rare worldview. Politicians of many stripes—Republican and Democrat, conservative, moderate, and liberal—strongly support charter schools. Presidents Clinton, Bush, and Obama and their education secretaries have been committed charter benefactors.

At the state and local levels, supporters include a diverse array of governors and state education chiefs, mayors and legislators, community-based organizations and superintendents. Charter supporters among the general public outnumber opponents by more than two to one.[26] Of course, many policies still disadvantage charters, but more and more these schools are seen as simply a different kind of public school.

Support for including private schools as equal partners in the K–12 establishment lags behind. But the trend is in the right direction. Publicly funded voucher programs exist in a number of cities, and their existence has been approved by the U.S. Supreme Court. They have been joined by a growing number of state tuition tax credit programs that accomplish the same goal of expanding choice into the private schools sector. But policy may be a lagging indicator of public sentiment. As former Chancellor Rhee's quotation shows, even those running large urban education bureaucracies can have an ecumenical position on school sector.

There are many examples of support for this unbiased approach among those working on the ground. A state-based education policy and advocacy leader wrote in language strikingly similar to Rhee: "We simply have too few schools—charters or district—that serve needy children in our urban areas well…In short, Ohio needs to embrace any and all schools that serve needy children well."[27]

A number of organizations are following this creed. Schools That Can provides assistance to a national set of high-performing schools in underserved communities, including charter, Lutheran, Catholic, and more. The REACH program in New York City helps low-income students in public, charter, and private schools thrive in high school, graduate, and succeed in college. In Cleveland, a group of the city's highest performing charters teamed with several outstanding Catholic schools to form a coalition designed to help expand the number of quality seats available in the city.

A 2010 survey of Philadelphia's parents conducted by the Pew Charitable Trusts found that parents aren't wedded to any of the three sectors. They think about individual schools—and nearly two-thirds of parents of district school students have actively considered transferring their children to charter or private schools.[28] In Detroit, a major cross-sector reform initiative was founded with the support of government, community, and philanthropic leaders. The philosophy of Excellent Schools Detroit is "to help all Detroit children, whether they happen to attend a traditional public school, public charter school, or independent school. Every child should be attending an excellent school, period."[29]

Despite this progress, more needs to be done to ingrain sector agnosticism into the conventional wisdom and public policy. Policies continue to treat differently schools operated by different entities. Areas of inequity include facilities, operational funding, assessments, accountability, and more. Practices regarding support for new schools, replications, and closures also vary drastically based on which sectors are at issue. And because these sectors are viewed differently by policymakers, each has developed its own advocacy apparatus, and these frequently work at cross-purposes.

The system spelled out in these pages would institutionalize the new approach by executing policies that treat all schools the same. They would all be evaluated based on quality, they would all be subject to the same standards and expectations, they would all have access to the same supports, and they would all have a fair opportunity to serve students.

Few would argue that America's inner-city kids are well served by today's delivery system of public education, a system that was created more than a century ago. This book has argued that meaningful, lasting improvement is within reach and that the principles of chartering hold the key. Though many still see chartering as just a way to start new schools or introduce greater accountability into public education, it has far greater contributions to make. It can fundamentally alter the way we manage portfolios of schools in urban America.

During its twenty years, chartering has proven itself to be fully compatible with our notions of public education. It has also fundamentally changed the thinking and practices of urban education leaders. As a result, at this point, the changes required to bring about the improvements we so desperately need are evolutionary not revolutionary. By fully committing to school quality and faithfully applying a series of strategies across the entire K–12 landscape, we have the potential to drastically improve the educational opportunities of our nation's most disadvantaged students.

Despite its humble beginnings in Minnesota two decades ago, chartering is now on the verge of helping us create a dynamic, responsive, high-performing, and self-improving system of schools: the urban school system of the future.

NOTES

1. Liz Bowie, "More Choices for Baltimore Eighth-graders," *Baltimore Sun*, January 3, 2010.

2. Sam Dillon, "Democrats Limit Future Financing for Washington Voucher Program," *New York Times*, February 27, 2009, sec. Education.

3. Joel Klein, "Official Transcript: Keynote, 2009 National Charter Schools Conference," Washington, DC, June 23, 2009, http://dashboard.publiccharters.org/KleinKeynoteNCSC09.

4. Klein, "Official Transcript: Keynote, 2009 National Charter Schools Conference."

5. *Losing Patience with Chronically Low-Performing Schools: How to Improve School Improvement*, Summary of a Public Hearing at Howard University, Blackburn Center Ballroom (Washington, DC: Commission on No Child Left Behind, September 2, 2009).

6. *The State of Public Education in New Orleans: Five Years after Hurricane Katrina* (New Orleans, LA: The Scott S. Cowen Institute for Public Education Initiatives at Tulane University, April 2009).

7. Paul Hill, et al., *Portfolio School Districts for Big Cities*, Interim Report (Bothell: Center for Reinventing Public Education, University of Washington, October 2009).

8. Joe Nathan, "Introduction," in *Public Schools by Choice: Expanding Opportunities for Parents, Students, and Teachers*, ed. Joe Nathan (Bloomington, IN: Meyer Share Books, 1989).

9. See Table 32-1 in *The Condition of Education* (Washington, DC: National Center for Education Statistics, Institute of Education Science, U.S. Department of Education, June 2009).

10. *The Condition of Education*, Table 6-1.

11. Mary Anne Raywid, "The Mounting Case for Schools of Choice," in *Public Schools by Choice*.

12. Charles Glenn, "Parent Choice and American Values," in *Public Schools by Choice*, 52.

13. Thomas Stewart, et al., *Family Reflections on the District of Columbia Opportunity Scholarship Program* (Fayetteville: School Choice Demonstration Project, University of Arkansas, January 2009).

14. Liz Bowie, "Exercising Choice," *Baltimore Sun*, Inside Ed, November 19, 2009.

15. Bowie, "More Choices for Baltimore Eighth-graders."

16. Thomas Stewart and Patrick J. Wolf, *Parent and Student Experiences with Choice in Milwaukee, Wisconsin*, SCDP Milwaukee Evaluation Report #13 (Fayetteville: School Choice Demonstration Project, University of Arkansas March 2009).

17. James VanderHoff, "Parental Valuation of Charter Schools and Student Performance," *Cato Journal* 28, no. 3 (Fall 2008): 479–93.

18. "Charter, Partnership and New Schools," The School District of Philadelphia website, http://webgui.phila.k12.pa.us/offices/c/charter-partnership-and-new-schools.

19. See "Schools in the Community: Portfolio and Planning," New York City Department of Education, http://schools.nyc.gov/community/planning/default.htm.

20. Baltimore City Public Schools, *Expanding Great Options SY 2010: Reviewing Schools to Maximize Success for Students*.

21. Glenn, "Parent Choice and American Values," 53.

22. For instance, see Javier C. Hernandez, "Three Schools Are Told They Will Be Shut Down," *New York Times*, December 4, 2008, sec. Education; Bill Turque, "District Proposes Closing 3 Schools," *Washington Post*, February 7, 2009.

23. Paul Tough, "A Teachable Moment," *The New York Times Magazine*, August 14, 2008.

24. Baltimore City Public Schools, *Expanding Great Options*.

25. Peggy Walsh-Sarnecki, "DPS Plans to close 29 schools," *Detroit Free Press*, May 12, 2009.

26. William Howell, Martin West, and Paul Peterson, "The Persuadable Public," *EducationNext* 9, no. 4 (Fall 2009).

27. Terry Ryan, "Let's Praise All Schools that Work as We Don't Have Enough of Them," *Flypaper*, August 28, 2009.

28. *Philadelphia's Changing Schools and What Parents Want from Them* (Philadelphia: Philadelphia Research Initiative, The Pew Charitable Trusts, June 2010).

29. "An Excellent School for Every Child in Detroit," *Excellent Schools Detroit*, June 5, 2010, http://www.excellentschoolsdetroit.org/.